PARENTS
&
PRODIGALS

DR. DOUGLAS E. CARR

Published by Doug Carr Freedom Ministry (DCFreedomMinistry)
Printed by Kindle Direct Publishing

ISBN: 978-1-7366952-7-2

Bible Translations Used

NKJV. Unless otherwise noted, Bible verses are from the NKJV. Scripture is taken from the New King James Version®. Copyright © 1982 by Thomas Nelson.

Other Bible Versions Used:

AMP. Copyright © 2015 by The Lockman Foundation, La Habra, CA 90631. All rights reserved.

KJV. King James Version. Scripture quotations marked "KJV" are taken from the Holy Bible, King James Version.

MSG. The Message. Copyright © 1993, 2002, 2018 by Eugene H. Peterson.

NIV. Holy Bible, New International Version®, NIV® Copyright ©1973, 1978, 1984, 2011 by Biblica, Inc.® Used by permission. All rights reserved worldwide.

NLT. New Living Translation (NLT) Holy Bible, New Living Translation, copyright © 1996, 2004, 2015 by Tyndale House Foundation. Used by permission of Tyndale House Publishers, Inc., Carol Stream, Illinois 60188. All rights reserved.

NLV. New Life Version (NLV) Copyright © 1969, 2003 by Barbour Publishing, Inc.

Endorsements

I believe the release of this book, Parents & Prodigals, is timely. Our/God's prodigals are at a Right Now Time (horaios- #5611) in the Greek from the Strong's Exhaustive Concordance) means belonging to the right hour or season or high time. Let us make the most of this Time, align with our Father's heart and wisdom and wage a good warfare on their behalf and see our/God's prodigals come home to the (Zoe) life that God has intended for each of them.

Ina Carr, fellow worker of the kingdom of God

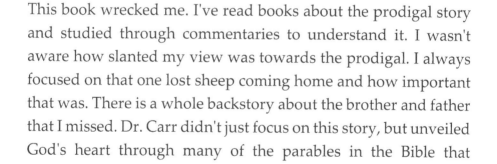

This book wrecked me. I've read books about the prodigal story and studied through commentaries to understand it. I wasn't aware how slanted my view was towards the prodigal. I always focused on that one lost sheep coming home and how important that was. There is a whole backstory about the brother and father that I missed. Dr. Carr didn't just focus on this story, but unveiled God's heart through many of the parables in the Bible that expresses the message of the family of prodigals, the actions needed, the wisdom used and why. The book will give you a greater understanding of God's word and perspective.

As I read through the pages, I found myself in the role of each character in the story. I've been in the shoes of the characters in different ways, in different times in my life. I've never had a book take me through God speaking to me and showing me His compassion not just for others but for me.

I don't care what you have or have not walked through in life, this book will change you and mark you in a way that will strengthen and build you to take this world on, believe for others, and be confident that God is able to save us all. I lack words to say how impactful this book was. I'm going back to read it a third time and take notes on what God is speaking to me.

I thought of so many leaders who have preached on the prodigal or are wanting to do it because this is the season of time where they will be coming home. Read this book! It's the richest, deepest understanding I've been able to access; it will wreck you—in a good way.

Cindy Williams Moore,
Pray Michigan! & MIAPC Leader/Founder

Watching children, friends, or family members drift away from their relationship with Jesus and fall into sin can be devastating. It leaves a heaviness and burden in our spirits and hearts that can at times feel debilitating. It can leave us feeling grieved and fearful of what these prodigal's eternity may look like if they don't repent and return to God. When we lose someone, we care about to sin, we can either try to win them back in our own strength, which can often make it worse, or we can war for their souls according to God's word.

In Parents & Prodigals, Dr Douglas Carr outlines the perfect battle strategy for winning our prodigals back and it starts with cleaning up our own hearts so we can be effective in interceding powerfully for the lost. Doug encourages with these words, "What do you think would happen if small groups of parents of prodigals would gather in prayer each week and simply agree in prayer for each other's wayward children... to see what God might do through Matthew 18:18-20 praying." Every chapter of Parents & Prodigals is packed with scripture and ends with prayers and activations that are certain to move God's heart and shift things in the spiritual realm!

Kimberly Burch
Youth Pastor
Overseer, Intercessory Prayer Team
LifeHouse Ministries

Contents

Dedication

I dedicate this book to the Good Shepherd, The Lord Jesus Christ, and to Abba Father. I personally was far from God until I was saved on March 17, 1972. My parents began attending a Liturgical Church before I began Junior High. I learned forms of religion but never knew the power of God. Other than that, I never entered a church until my cousin Greg's funeral. He was older than me and was killed along with several other teenagers when a drunk ran into them as they were returning home from a movie. About all I remember is the confusion after the funeral. My grandmother said God took him so he wouldn't have to go to Vietnam. Even in my lostness, I knew that did not line up with who God really is. On the way home I listened to my parents berate the priest who officiated the service. I determined I would never be involved in ministry. Our God laughs.

In 1987, after fourteen years of full-time ministry and seventeen years of marriage, my prodigal heart was exposed. I had become proud, religious, and a workaholic. Succumbing to the stress of building a new church, teaching Sunday School, preaching Sunday morning, evening, and Wednesday nights. Being principal of our Christian School, helping direct band, choirs, leading morning devotions and Wednesday chapel, I was proud of working 70-80 weeks. I did not realize I was trying to win Father' God's approval.

On Father's Day weekend, 1987, my first wife had enough of playing second fiddle with everything else in my life. She left and I ended up being custodial parent of our three children. We made a few attempts at reconciliation, but called it quits one disastrous weekend in August.

I did not think God could ever use me again. I called the primary leaders of our church that night and resigned immediately. I had been taught ministers who go through divorce should never pastor again. Having been married since age 18, and in ministry since age 22, I thought I was done forever.

Being a husband, preacher and parent was not something I did. It was who I was. I lost my identity and I fell back into worldly values and sin. I continued going to church, trying twenty-six different churches over the next five years. I was seeking unconditional love, acceptance, and forgiveness but could not find it. Most of them did not have use for a "used-up" backslidden preacher.

Thankfully, Abba Father kept watching for this backslidden son to return home. The party He threw for me continues to this day. I never knew, acknowledged, or accepted His love, acceptance, and forgiveness until I returned to Father God who is represented by the prodigal son's father.

I dedicate this book to Him.

Acknowledgments

In all things I recognize my precious wife of nearly thirty years. She breathes life, inspiration, grace, and mercy into everything we do. She exemplifies the heart of The Father. She offers her all in serving the Lord, me, our church, and family. She leads us into breakthrough worship week after week. All who enter in are blessed, renewed, and sent out in the love, power, acceptance, and forgiveness of God. She also preaches at least once a month.

Suzanne LeBlanc continues diligently volunteering her skills to edit my books even with the burden of caring for her mother who lives with Suzanne. Her mother has been in and out of the hospital regularly over the past few years. Her mental, physical, and emotional health has declined so in recent years that taking care of her takes herculean effort from Suzanne, even while she works a very demanding job from home.

Suzanne continues editing my books, creating wonderful Power Points for my messages each week, and helping me and others better fulfil our roles in the Kingdom of God.

Barbara De Simon, of Rooted Publishing Service created the cover for this book and oversees the uploading and publishing on Kindle Direct. With her expertise, she saves me hours.

His House Foursquare Church continues to support and encourage me, even when authoring books and leading Doug Carr Freedom Ministry cuts into my time.

With so much help and encouragement, I am able to accomplish more than seems humanly possible. I acknowledge them all.

Foreword by Stan Dudka

Too often, people face many challenges when it comes to processing all the aspects of having prodigals in their lives. They hear sermon after sermon and teaching after teaching about prodigals, but those leave them with little strategy as to how to approach it all. As parents of prodigals, they are left to deal with their blame, disappointment, and shame. The prodigal is left to deal with their choice and all the fallout of that. Is there a road of restoration? Is there a road for parents to take?

Dr. Doug Carr has taken on the challenge of this book with The Fear of the Lord and seeking The Wisdom of the Lord. His feet wanted to run from writing this book, but his heart knew there was a yes deep in there. There are so many different layers to the heart of the prodigal as well as many layers to the heart of the parent. Dr. Carr shows us the layers to the love in the Father's Heart.

Dr. Carr uses a tapestry of Scripture to create a road map of strategy for prayer and Warring in Prayer and for Deliverance and for Restoration. This Scripture rich writing goes up and beyond other writings on or near this subject. Sometimes authors give you a new lens of insight into a subject. Dr. Carr has created many layers of lens to open the reader's eyes and heart to new understanding.

Whatever aspect or side or person you find yourself relating to in the Biblical account of the Prodigal Son story, Dr. Carr has given you a new place to look from, a place full of wisdom, insight and Scripture. May the Lord bless you on this journey called a book.

Pastor Stan Dudka
Voice ministries
58247 Crossview Lane
Osceola, IN 46561
info@voiceministries.com

Foreword by Keri Warren

In this book, author Douglas Carr presents an in-depth exploration of one of the most familiar parables in the Bible, the Prodigal Son. He astutely discusses two other parables to enhance its significance: The lost sheep and the lost coin. These parables demonstrate how Jesus places special priority on bringing people that are lost back to him. In reviewing these parables, Dr. Carr cleverly reveals the nature of God through careful examination of how the father responds to his two sons: one wayward and reckless, the other obedient, though eventually resentful, and jealous. Any of us who have prodigal children will receive excellent guidance from the manner in which Dr. Carr portrays these parables. He contrasts the importance of true love, a love that sometimes requires firmness, coupled with forgiveness and compassion, as expressed by the father, and compares it to the reaction of the older son, who becomes angry when the father celebrates the long-awaited return of his son with a fatted calf. On a practical level, Dr. Carr helps parents to understand that true love sometimes requires tough love. No parent likes to see a son, or a daughter suffer. But because God gives all people free will, some children choose their own path of rebellion or make bad choices that result in painful consequences. To minimize the suffering of such consequences, some parents rescue their children, falsely believing that they are responding out of love. However, these rescuing behaviors are harmful and enabling and they minimize any hope for true repentance and genuine change. Dr. Carr illustrates how the father demonstrates tough love. He lets his son go and allows him to experience the consequences of his choices. Through suffering, the son repents and returns home where his father greets him with genuine love and deep compassion. Likewise, when parents resist the temptation to rescue their children, choosing instead to tolerate the discomfort felt as their children suffer the consequences, God can do the deeper transformative work that promotes true repentance, humility, and genuine changes of the heart. And, if parents are burdened with guilt because they inadvertently contributed to the behaviors of the child, they can forgive themselves and extend that same loving forgiveness and compassion to their children as they wait on God, give Him glory, and rejoice over the anticipated return of the prodigal.

Keri Warren, PhD, LPC, NCC, LMFT
Individual, Couples & Family Counseling
Certified Spiritual Director, DMin
1945 Pauline Blvd., Suite 10
Ann Arbor, Michigan 48103
KareCounseling.com

Author's Preface

I became a Christian at a Basic Youth Conflicts Seminar in 1972. Since then I have attended Christian conferences and trainings in a variety of settings.

One common denominator I've witnessed among preachers, teachers, and fellow Believers is the heart-tug felt whenever a speaker addresses prodigal children.

I have pastored since 1976 in different circles. Countless parents have requested prayers for their prodigal children. I've had prodigals in my own family as well.

God called me to write a sermon series on prodigals and their parents. It was a challenge, but well worth the effort. In this book I share a lot of what God taught me as I studied the plight of prodigals for five months.

There are two major groups who are unlikely to see prodigals come home whole and sound. The first group is parents who have simply quit caring, if indeed, they ever did. The second group is those who care too much and err on the side of such great compassion they do not leave room for the Lord to teach their prodigals the lessons they must learn.

I write from the background of a parent, grandparent, great-great grandparent, pastor, author, and freedom minister. I do not pretend to have all the answers. I do hope, however, to stimulate thinking and prayer for prodigals and those who love them.

May God be your teacher and guide as you work through this book on the behalf of those you love who have gone astray.

Chapter One:
The Greatest Measure of Love is God's Love for Prodigals!

Stan Dudka of Voice Ministries heard of the vision I carry for this book and suggested the title should be the same as the title of this chapter. I wrestled with different titles, beginning with "Parents of Prodigals," then Stan's suggestion, and finally settling on Parents & Prodigals, leaving room for Stan's suggestion as a chapter heading and for use in the foreword he offered to write.

There are three things I know about God concerning every prodigal child: God loves them even more than we do.

The true value of anything is determined by what people are willing to pay for it. My wife and I enjoy going to garage sales and occasional auctions. We are amazed how some people pay large sums for something we won't even make a bid on. What they are willing to pay shows the item's value in the eyes of the purchaser. The Bible clearly states how much prodigals are worth to Father God. He was willing to give His only begotten Son to purchase their redemption.

I saw a Gospel Tract depicting a down and out person who asked Jesus how much He loved them. Jesus stretched out His nail scarred hands and said, "This much."

📖 For God so loved the world that He gave His only begotten Son, that whoever believes in Him should not perish but have everlasting life. [17] For God did not send His Son into the world to condemn the world, but that the world through Him might be saved. John 3:16–17.

Father God wants your prodigal saved even more than you do!

📖 The Lord is not slack concerning *His* promise, as some count slackness, but is longsuffering toward us, not willing that any should perish but that all should come to repentance. 2 Peter 3:9.

Father God knows best what it takes to reach prodigals.

Allow me to share some tidbits from Psalm 65. I add my thoughts in italics within parentheses.

📖 Seek the Lord while He may be found, *(There is a kairos time, times that present the best opportunities to be found of the Lord)* Call upon Him while He is near. *(There is a time of God's close Presence we must not miss.)* [7] Let the wicked forsake his way, *(There is a call to repent.)* And the unrighteous man his thoughts; *(Repent: "met-an-eh'-o" – To think differently or afterwards, i.e., reconsider; morally, feel compunction: repent)* Let him return to the Lord, And He will have mercy on him; And to our God, For He will abundantly pardon. Isaiah 55:6–7. Author's comments in parenthesis.

Parents and friends of prodigals must come into agreement with God's Thoughts for them.

📖 "For My thoughts *are* not your thoughts, Nor *are* your ways My ways," says the Lord. [9] "For *as* the heavens are higher than the earth, So are My ways higher than your ways, And My thoughts than your thoughts. Isaiah 55:8–9.

As we strive to restore prodigals, we must grasp how much greater God's thinking is compared to our thinking. I wrote the book *God's Say So versus Man's Know So,*[1] in 2015. It compares what the Bible says to what people "know" concerning topics like sexuality, home life, pornography, theft, sanctity of marriage and sanctity of life, gambling, etc. Unfortunately, many are not concerned what God knows, because they think they know it all.

The Lord planted the seed of this book in my heart several months before I began writing. I was not in a hurry to develop it, for fear my motive might be suspect. Well-meaning people who try to help people are often judged as being critical and judgmental. Indeed, some people *are* critical and judgmental, but I pray what I share will be received as from one delivered from a critical spirit.

Parents often take offense even when sincere friends or pastors dare suggest their child has a problem. There is no such fury as a bear robbed of her cubs, or as the Bible states it,

📖 Let a man meet a bear robbed of her cubs, Rather than a fool in his folly. Proverbs 17:12.

People are prone to getting uptight if they even suspect someone is criticizing them for their parenting skills or judging their children or grandchildren for improper behavior. The devil tricks some into becoming furious and irrational if they think you are judging *them* because of how their descendants behave.

I have a pastor's heart and truly care for people, yet I have been judged because I sincerely try to help them or their children. They miss what Jesus wants His Body to be and do. He wants us to be on mission together to rescue prodigals.

Although I agree with very little some politicians say, I partly agree with. "It takes a village to raise a child." Better yet, it takes a Church family to rear parents and children. For now, I promise I am not judging or condemning parents or their children. I've learned hindsight is better than foresight. How I wish I had known when my children were young the things I now hope to share. I'm still learning and growing.

Jesus does not call His **Ekklesia*** to be wishy washy about things affecting the eternal destiny of children or adults. But this is not the main focus of this chapter. Focus here, however.

***Ekklesia** is the Greek term Jesus used. It is often translated "church," which gives a picture of the building where people worship. In the Greek Language of the New Testament, it refers to a called-out assembly with the assignment to advance the Kingdom of God in all the world. I use the original Greek name and definition Jesus used for His called-out body here and primarily through my writing.)

Herein, I share God-given Scriptural insight concerning parents and prodigals. Problems seldom resolve themselves if we ignore them. For the Ekklesia to be what Christ Jesus intends it to be, there are times we must put on our big girl and big boy pants, refuse to be offended, and trust friends who love us enough to share the concerns God leads them to share. It is time to believe the Bible enough to accept what it says.

📖 Open rebuke *is* better than love carefully concealed. [6] Faithful *are* the wounds of a friend, but the kisses of an enemy *are* deceitful. Proverbs 27:5–6.

I would rather be rebuked by someone who loves me and my children, than be kissed by an enemy. How about you? Many of us have prodigal children and/or grandchildren. My children were brought up in a pastor's home, grew up in Church, were privileged to attend a Christian School for nine years, but they are not all as close to Jesus and His Ekklesia as I wish them to be. Many parents of prodigals testify their child's friendship with the world has moved beyond backsliding to being prodigals. God has prompted me to approach this subject:

How to help prodigals without enabling them.

This message is beyond the scope of my knowledge and understanding. It is something I cannot share apart from God's wisdom and revelation. I seek His inspiration, anointing, revelation, and grace as I share what He has put on my heart.

God's thumb became increasingly heavy as I sensed His pressure to write a message for parents and prodigals. I write to myself first and to you secondly. I thought I could put it off a bit longer because I was working on another book, *Equipping Children for Kingdom Advance* which was easier to write. "Not so," said the Lord. I came face to face, so to speak, with Him on my prayer walk early January 2023. Later, He interrupted my daily prayer time in the office and again applied loving pressure to begin a series of messages which was foundational for this book. In my Daily Listening Room, He spoke the following words I share with you now.

Son, you know in your heart I want you to teach on Parents and Prodigals. You are writing this book for Me. I AM giving it for parents, young and old, who have prodigals and simply do not know what to do. They love their children and grandchildren like I love Jesus. I willingly sacrificed Him, temporarily, that others might be with Me for eternity. He is the First Fruit of millions whom I will usher into the place I have prepared for them. Had I not entrusted My son to be attacked by the devil, scorned of men, and brutally ravaged by religious and political persecution unto death, there would be no salvation for mankind. He continued, *I had to let go and let My Son Jesus, as God and man, to be subject to all He endured in order that He might win for humanity the goal of abundant and eternal life.*

He faced pain that all might gain.

My heart in this message will help parents seek My face in the midst of the pain of prodigal children. As they do so, their children might gain salvation and life more abundantly.

No discipline seems pleasant at the time, but in the end, it leads to a harvest of righteousness and peace for those who have been trained by it. It is a mistake to remove wayward children from my training. Father God. He then added,

"Oh, to be like me," means fully entrusting your child to Me."

A common definition of parables is, "a parable is an earthly story with a heavenly meaning." God further expanded that definition of Parable as thus:

Every parable in the Bible is an earthly story inspired by God to bring heavenly insight to those so earthly, they might miss heaven's message apart from worldly illustrations.

God is concerned about lost people and the people who love them. As we seek God, His Word, His revelation, and insight, we will gain understanding of how to effectively reach prodigals. That is what Luke 15 is all about.

We must grasp the buried treasure God placed in the parables of the lost sheep, the lost coin, and the lost son. Unfortunately, this will not come without resistance. Satan does not want prodigals to return home.

I know a lovely couple who were pastoring a church. People— singles, couples and families started flocking in. Some of the old guard did not like the growth and all the noisy children coming to church. To make a long story short, my friends and these seekers became victims of corporate spirits of religion. People under their control use boards, committees, arguments, surveys and the like to stop the good work God was doing in and for people who were getting saved and becoming true disciples. Religious people are more concerned about keeping things "decently in order" than they are in helping people who might create messes or be a little noisy. God wants us to share His unconditional love, acceptance, and forgiveness with prodigals.

**Religious people complain about the lengths
People are willing to go to reach the lost.**

Luke 15 addresses a lost sheep, a lost coin, and a lost son, but it begins with religious people criticizing Jesus for keeping company with the prodigals who needed Him most.

📖 Then all the tax collectors and the sinners drew near to Him to hear Him. ² And the Pharisees and scribes complained, saying, "This Man receives sinners and eats with them." Luke 15:1–2.

These self-righteous, religious phonies criticized Jesus for reaching out to those who most needed Him! Such resistance is religious, not grace or mercy.

Years ago, I helped launch a bus ministry in a respectable denominational church. Though the church people there were gracious, I was shocked and embarrassed when I discovered how challenging and disruptive unchurched youth can be.

Those children got up whenever they felt like it to walk the halls. They talked during church. God used that to give me my first teaching ministry. I launched Jr. Church so we could continue reaching lost children without totally disturbing our morning services. Aren't children—including prodigal sons and daughters worth the effort of cleaning up some messes so we can rescue them from the messed-up lives they have experienced?

— C.T. Studd said, "Some want to live within the sound of church or chapel bell; I want to run a rescue shop, within a yard of hell." He also said, "Only one life, 'twill soon be past, Only what's done for Christ will last." Studd lived from 1860–1931 and was a British Missionary. He is also remembered for his skills in sports like cricket and bowling. But his greatest passion was loving Jesus and those Jesus loves, including prodigals, the lost, and misguided. Studd shared the heart of the Good Shepherd. He became a missionary to China and help set up the Heart of Africa Mission. He was willing to give his all to rescue the lost from the burning fires of hell and to bring prodigals to their fulness in Christ.

So, with that long introduction, we will peer into God's heart for lost sheep, lost wealth, and take a sneak peek at lost children.

Take a moment to ask Holy Spirit: "What are you saying to me through this chapter?" Jot down any thoughts He gives you and pray; make them a matter of prayer and meditation.

Prayer: Father, I ask You to give me the grace and power to love prodigals and their parents like You love me. Help me accept and walk in your love and let it flow through me to those who most need you. In Jesus' Name, Amen.

Footnotes:

[1] Douglas Carr, *God's Say So versus Man's Know So*. Create Space, 2015.

Chapter Two: The Lost Sheep

Jesus is the Good Shepherd. His sheep are those who follow Him and listen to His voice.

📖 So He spoke this parable to them, saying: ⁴"What man of you, having a hundred sheep, if he loses one of them, does not leave the ninety-nine in the wilderness, and go after the one which is lost until he finds it? ⁵And when he has found *it*, he lays *it* on his shoulders, rejoicing. ⁶And when he comes home, he calls together *his* friends and neighbors, saying to them, 'Rejoice with me, for I have found my sheep which was lost!' ⁷I say to you that likewise there will be more joy in heaven over one sinner who repents than over ninety-nine just persons who need no repentance. Luke 15:3–7.

Good Shepherds go to great lengths to restore lost sheep to the sheepfold.

In the natural world, when a sheep strays to dangerous areas, all a shepherd usually must do is love them back to a safe place. Some sheep, however, require far greater intervention to be guided back to a safe environment.

Sheep who were rejected by their mother need far more effort and consideration. Occasionally, when an ewe gives birth to a lamb, she rejects it. She won't allow it to nurse or accept it in any way. These rejected lambs are called "bummer lambs."

Such rejection not only puts them on the path to starvation, but also breaks their spirit. They stand with heads laid low.

Shepherds carefully watch for these little lambs. A good shepherd will find the bummer lamb, hold it close to his heart so it can hear his heartbeat, and take it home. He cuddles it, bottle feeds it, and keeps it warm.

Throughout the days ahead, the shepherd continues to carry the lamb close to his heart. He knows it needs nurturing or it will die of a broken spirit. As the lamb rests near his heart, it learns the sound of his voice. Slowly it begins to trust the good shepherd.

By the time a bummer lamb is ready to be released back into the flock, the little lamb has a new dignity. It no longer feels rejected. It feels special and holds its head high. It has been singled out by the shepherd. When the shepherd calls his sheep, the bummer lambs are always the first who come running. Such is Jesus' heart for lost sheep, and lost sons and daughters.

The focus here is on the sheep and not on the shepherd.

It is much easier to rescue "bummer lambs" than it is unmanageable sheep. Rebellious sheep need far stricter training. When a sheep refuses to stay within the safe boundaries established by the shepherd, more drastic action is needed. There are extreme times when a shepherd must break a sheep's leg to keep it from running away from the flock into danger.

While breaking a sheep's leg may seem barbaric, it was done for the welfare of the sheep.

If allowed to run wild, the sheep might pasture on poisonous plants or run away to danger from predators like wolves. Breaking the leg of a wandering sheep, kept it from running from the flock! The broken leg protected it from harm. Since a sheep with a broken leg cannot walk, the shepherd carries it close to his chest until its mended leg healed. Once healed, the sheep wants to stay near the shepherd.

Luke 19:1–10 speaks of the criticism Jesus' faced when he visited Zacchaeus' House. Zacchaeus was the short little tax collector who climbed up a sycamore tree to catch a glimpse of Jesus when He passed by. Jesus did not invite Zacchaeus to the synagogue. Instead, He invited Himself to "Zach's" house, where He dined with tax collectors and sinners. He was criticized by the religious phonies for His efforts, even though Jesus' efforts led to Zacchaeus's repentance and to restoring everything he had wrongly taken, plus giving half his goods to the poor. Like C. T. Studd, Jesus' love for the people who needed Him most compelled Him to take action on their behalf.

Consider Jesus' response to the one who criticized him for hanging out with tax collectors and sinners.

📖 And Jesus said to him, "Today salvation has come to this house, because he also is a son of Abraham; 10 for the Son of Man has come to seek and to save that which was lost." Luke 19:9–10.

Jesus is concerned for prodigals. He is their only answer.

Take a moment to ask Holy Spirit: "What are you saying to me through this chapter?" Jot down any thoughts He gives you and pray; make them a matter of prayer and meditation.

Prayer: Jesus, I ask You to give me Your heart for prodigals. Release Your love for them to me so I might see beyond their limitations and have a glimpse of Your love, calling, and purpose for their lives. Amen.

Chapter Three: The Lost Coin

In Luke 15:8–9, Jesus used a simple materialistic coin to demonstrate God's heart for prodigals and sinners.

📖 "Or what woman, having ten silver coins, if she loses one coin, does not light a lamp, sweep the house, and search carefully until she finds *it?* ⁹ And when she has found *it,* she calls *her* friends and neighbors together, saying, 'Rejoice with me, for I have found the piece which I lost!' Luke 15:8–9.

It is always a blessing to stumble over blessings. They are reminder of how God is aware of what we are going through and is ready to come to our aid. The first chapter of my book, *Ancient Keys Special Names of Jehovah*[1], is "El Roi, the God who sees our need and comes to our aid." El Roi is first mentioned in Genesis 16 when Hagar was running from Abram and Sarai and had run out of provision. She feared her son was going to die when El Roi showed up and met their need in the nick of time.

Pam and I witnessed the work of El Roi in a small, yet large way one memorable weekend. We had a snowstorm on December 25, 2022. We were among a handful who made it to church that day, either because of the storm or because it was Christmas Day.

Long story short: the offering was so low we did not get paid. We had been given a gift certificate for McDonalds, so the following Saturday we went to McDonalds for breakfast. I was opening the car door for my wife when I "just happened" to see a blessing God had prepared for us. I noticed a $20 bill, weathered from the snowplows, pressed against the curb where we parked. We considered it a gift from the Lord. Then, just before going to bed I did some heart-to-heart listening with Pam concerning a struggle she was having about a man who falsely accused her. I checked my phone when we were done talking and saw a PayPal notice of a gift of $1,000 from a family we ministered to earlier that year. What a wonderful "find." Like the widow of Zarephath, we rejoiced! But there is more to the widow's story.

In the first parable of Luke 15, a woman lost one of her ten silver coins. This woman turned her attention from the nine coins (They may represent children.) she still had and turned her focus to finding the one coin (child) that was lost.

Sandy Williams, a long-standing member of our church, mentioned something I had not heard, so I looked it up. Not only were the coins valuable, but women were often given ten silver coins as a wedding gift or dowry. Each coin, a drachma, was worth a day's wage. The coins were often set in a necklace. Since there were ten coins, they were the sum of what one earned in two five-day workweeks. When worn on a necklace, they displayed marital covenant like wedding rings do now. Having one coin missing would be like losing a diamond in an engagement or wedding ring. It is no wonder the woman rejoiced when she found the lost coin.

As I mentioned earlier, the lost coin might represent prodigal children. Even a person blessed with ten children will do everything they can to bring one prodigal home.

The pain caused by prodigals is deeper than losing valuable jewelry. The book of wisdom compares the value of grandfathers and grandchildren to jewels in a crown.

📖 Like jewels in a crown, **"Children's children *are* the crown of old men, and the glory of children *is* their father."** Proverbs 17:6.

Unfortunately, that is the way God designed family life to be, but often that is not the way it truly is. The glory of many children is not their father. Grandchildren often bring disgrace to their Grandparents. As we all know, there aren't any perfect grandparents, parents, or children. Only a few fathers or sons are the best of the best. Still, God has a redemptive plan for any who will surrender fully to Him and His ways.

When a person has multiple children, even if only one is a prodigal, it can suck the glory from the rest of the family. I think of a dear woman who lost a daughter to an overdose. The loss stole her peace and blessedness for some time.

The devil is after children and prodigals. I recently prayed with Pastor Bob Renner who does jail ministry in Centreville. He told me there were three men who were released from jail in the previous month who had already committed suicide or overdosed on Fentanyl. We must do our best to reach prodigals quickly. Drugs are killing far too many of our sons and daughters.

As Jesus concludes the parable of the lost coin, He again emphasizes His right heart toward tax collectors and sinners who are worth far more than a lost coin. They are worth searching for until they are found. There should be a call for celebration when they are found and returned to their place in the home. Verse 10 sums it up.

📖 Likewise, I say to you, there is joy in the presence of the angels of God over one sinner who repents." Luke 15:10.

Do you want to make heaven happy? Do what you can to restore prodigals! Which child are parents most concerned for? Usually, it is the prodigal. Who do they pray and weep over the most? Who robs them of restful sleep and wearies them to the point they cannot sleep. Usually, it is the child who has strayed the furthest away from their love and care.

Prodigals are worth whatever it takes to win them back.

One huge variant between a lost sheep, a lost coin, and a lost son is sheep are so driven by instinct they require close shepherding to keep them safe. Coins are totally dependent on whether or not humans use them and protect them. Sheep have instincts, but they can also be trained in positive or negative ways to become accepted or rejected, loved or unloved, etc.

People, on the other hand, are free to make choices that bring either blessing or curse. Humans, more than any other creature, have free wills. Their freedom or captivity, and success or failure, is largely dependent upon their personal choices, regardless of how they have been treated. People always have freedom to choose how to live. (God will not remove their free will, and we certainly cannot remove it!)

One definition of prodigal is "spending money or resources freely and recklessly: wastefully extravagant." Think of how much drugs, alcohol, tobacco, and vaping products cost. I read an article in the Sturgis Journal, titled *Michigan's cannabis industry outlook for '23*. It tells how competition from increasing numbers of pot shops has brought prices of recreational marijuana down 50% from the price in November 2021 to $95.12 an ounce in November 2022.[2] I had no idea one ounce of marijuana cost that much.

Prodigals hurt themselves and those who love them.

Even so, Jesus gave the parables of the lost sheep and the lost coin to emphasize our need to seek prodigals and rejoice when they are found.

Take a moment to ask Holy Spirit: "What are you saying to me through this chapter?" Jot down any thoughts He gives you and pray; make them a matter of prayer and meditation.

Prayer: Father, Son, and Holy Spirit, please help me understand how the parables of the lost sheep and the lost coin apply to me and those I love. Show me how You want me to respond to prodigals and how to support those who love them. Amen.

Footnotes:

[1] Douglas E. Carr, *Ancient Keys Special Names of Jehovah*, KDP 2020.

[2] *Michigan's cannabis industry outlook for '23*. Adrienne Roberts, January 12, 2023, Sturgis Journal.

Chapter Four: The Parable of the Lost Son

This chapter serves as a brief introduction to what is called The Parable of the Lost Son. This is the foundation and heart of the study which follows.

All Scripture is inspired of God and useful for and *is* profitable for doctrine, for reproof, for correction, for instruction in righteousness (2 Timothy 3:16). Later the modern chapter divisions were added around A.D. 1227. Verse numbers were later added to the Old Testament in A.D. 1488 and the New Testament in 1555.

People divided the Books of the Bible into chapters and verses to make them easier to reference.

There was a lot of perspiration in their work, but little inspiration. Later, people added titles to sections of Scripture. Men added three titles in Luke 15. They are in bold print in my Bible: The Parable of the Lost Sheep, The Parable of the Lost Coin, and the Parable of the Lost Son. Such titles are helpful for reference, but they are not inspired.

We usually focus more on the prodigal than we do on the prodigal's father. This is unfortunate, because we won't find the answers we need by focusing on lost sheep, lost coins, or lost children. The fact they are lost reveals they do not have the answer. Neither do we. We need God's help!

It is imperative we grasp the heavenly emphasis of the earthly stories of the lost sheep, the lost coin, and the lost son. God wants us to see how the Good Shepherd restored the lost son. His light shines on the effort a woman was willing to make to ransom her lost coin. God also wants us to see what the Father of the prodigal son did, and perhaps more importantly, what he did not do which led to his son returning home.

Interested? We will move into that topic in the next chapter. Please pray for me, yourselves, prodigal children, and their parents. God is up to something we do not want to miss.

In the next chapter, we will look at the Prodigal's Parent(s).

Take a moment to ask Holy Spirit: "What are you saying to me through this chapter?" Jot down any thoughts He gives you and pray; make them a matter of prayer and meditation.

Prayer: Heavenly Father, thank You for Your heart for prodigals, their parents, and children. We cry out to You! We open our hearts to Your heart. We open our spirits to receive revelation, insight, strategy, and tools to bring prodigals home to You and to our families. Amen.

Chapter Five: Parable of a Prodigal's Parent
A Parent's only Hope—God's Way

It might be helpful to study the Scriptures we will look at in your own Bible, phone, or computer and mark what God speaks to you through them. I also include them here for your reference. I challenge you to read each Scripture given. Eat and digest the Word of God and you will come to know the God of the Word more intimately. The first passage is long, but full of insight. I will give it in bite size portions. Luke 15:11–32.

📖 Then He said: "A certain man had two sons. ¹²And the younger of them said to *his* father, 'Father, give me the portion of goods that falls *to me.*' So he divided to them *his* livelihood. ¹³And not many days after, the younger son gathered all together, journeyed to a far country, and there wasted his possessions with prodigal living.

Prodigal living means wasteful living. Think of how prodigals waste their potential, money, etc. But this wasn't just any man or representative of all men. It was a certain man. This is important because every parent and child is unique in God's eyes. Each person has strong points and weak points.

📖 But when he had spent all, there arose a severe famine in that land, and he began to be in want. ¹⁵ Then he went and joined himself to a citizen of that country, and he sent him into his fields to feed swine. ¹⁶ And he would gladly have filled his stomach with the pods that the swine ate, and no one gave him *anything.*

This certain son had to reach the bottom of the barrel before he came to his senses.

📖 "But when he came to himself, he said, 'How many of my father's hired servants have bread enough and to spare, and I perish with hunger! ¹⁸ I will arise and go to my father, and will say to him, "Father, I have sinned against heaven and before you, ¹⁹ and I am no longer worthy to be called your son. Make me like one of your hired servants." '

Once this prodigal got to his lowest point, the only way to look was up. At this point, prodigals begin to realize how much their prodigal living is costing them.

📖 "And he arose and came to his father. But when he was still a great way off, his father saw him and had compassion, and ran and fell on his neck and kissed him. ²¹ And the son said to him, 'Father, I have sinned against heaven and in your sight, and am no longer worthy to be called your son.'

This prodigal had to take the first step. He personally had to turn and head back home. The Father's compassion made his return much easier.

📖 "But the father said to his servants, 'Bring out the best robe and put *it* on him, and put a ring on his hand and sandals on *his* feet. ²³ And bring the fatted calf here and kill *it,* and let us eat and be merry; ²⁴ for this my son was dead and is alive again; he was lost and is found.' And they began to be merry.

Every true return of a prodigal deserves celebration.

📖 "Now his older son was in the field. And as he came and drew near to the house, he heard music and dancing. ²⁶ So he called one of the servants and asked what these things meant. ²⁷ And he said to him, 'Your brother has come, and because he has received him safe and sound, your father has killed the fatted calf.'

There are usually good and compassionate responses to the return of a prodigal. There may also be negative and critical reactions.

📖 "But he was angry and would not go in. Therefore his father came out and pleaded with him. ²⁹ So he answered and said to *his* father, 'Lo, these many years I have been serving you; I never transgressed your commandment at any time; and yet you never gave me a young goat, that I might make merry with my friends. ³⁰ But as soon as this son of yours came, who has devoured your livelihood with harlots, you killed the fatted calf for him.'

An important choice awaits the return of every prodigal. Will there be acceptance and forgiveness, or judgment, rejection, and bitterness?

📖 ³¹ "And he said to him, 'Son, you are always with me, and all that I have is yours. ³² It was right that we should make merry and be glad, for your brother was dead and is alive again, and was lost and is found.' " Luke 15:11–32.

Amen! In Paul's first letter to Timothy, he shares how all Scripture, including the long one from Luke, is useful for helping us as we attempt to others.

📖 All Scripture *is* given by inspiration of God, and is profitable for doctrine, for reproof, for correction, for instruction in righteousness, [17] that the man of God may be complete, thoroughly equipped for every good work.
2 Timothy 3:16–17.

Every word God put in the Bible is trustworthy for life and practice. God warns we should never add or subtract anything from the Bible (Revelation 22:18–19). I do not believe the Lord scorns adding chapter and verse numbers to the Scripture for reference's sake. Nor do section headings, notes or footnotes desecrate the Word of God. Still, we must note that only the words God put in Scripture are inspired and trustworthy. Not so the chapter divisions, notes, or titles placed over sections of Scripture.

Strong's Greek Concordance on Matthew 16:18 gives the accurate translation as Ekklesia, not church.

ἐκκλησίαν (ekklēsian) Noun - Accusative Feminine Singular. Strong's Greek 1577: From a compound of ek and a derivative of kaleo; a calling out, i.e., a popular meeting, especially a religious congregation.

Recently I listened to a wonderful message by Eric Neal Moore (Cindy Williams Moore's husband). He said "Ekklesia is the accurate word often mistranslated "church." It refers to the called-out assembly of Believers Jesus told Peter the gates of hell could not prevail against. Eric explained King James was threatened by the thought of an Ekklesia of Kingdom people reigning in his territory, so one of his demands was Ekklesia be translated as Church in the King James Bible.

Now, look at the heading just before Luke 15:11. "The Parable of the Lost Son." That heading is not inspired.

It was a human addition—not a God addition.

It switches the whole focus to the problem rather than the solution. It focuses on the lost younger brother who wanted to grab all the gusto he could and the sorry predicament he got himself into. We don't need an in-depth study of the prodigal son. We have an abundance of prodigals in our church families and our own families.

In the last chapter, I gave this definition of prodigal, "Spending "money or resources freely and recklessly: wastefully extravagant." Prodigals not only waste their own resources but those of caring family, churches, and society. In 2018 the expense of lodging a prisoner was $36,299.25 a year or $99.45 a day! This is only the cost of incarceration. It does not tally the costs of prodigals who are not in prison. I don't know how to estimate the cost of prodigals who rely on others for health care, welfare, housing, food, clothing and the like.

Looking at general statistics is bad enough. Counting the cost of prodigals to parents, spouses, and extended family can be mind boggling. Society invests millions of dollars studying homelessness and hunger. They may state etymologies of such problems, but they are short of solutions. Perhaps it is time to come back to the Word of God and the God of the Word. If we need a heading for Luke 15:11–32, I suggest we take our focus off the prodigal and put it on the One who has the answers.

A better heading for Luke 15:11–32 is:
The Parable of Parents of Prodigals.

In this infamous story of the prodigal son, the three main characters are the father, the older son, and the younger son. The earthly father represents our Heavenly Father. The older son represents the Jews, and the younger son represents the Gentiles.

The Father of the prodigal son represents Heavenly Father.

The focus is on God the Father, who so loved the world, He willingly surrendered His only begotten Son, so whoever believes in Him should not perish but have everlasting life (John 3:16).

I first memorized John 3:16 in the KJV.

📖 For God so loved the world, that he gave his only begotten Son, that **whosoever** believeth in him should not perish, but have everlasting life. John 3:16. KJV.

"Whosoever" clearly presents choice and consequence.

Those who choose to believe in and follow Christ Jesus will not perish but have life more abundantly. God never removes freedom of choice from humans. Prodigals are free to turn to God or reject Him. They are not, however, free of the consequences of their decisions, particularly, their wrong decisions. God holds each prodigal personally accountable. The proverbial Father of the prodigal son represents God the Father, who knows best. Following His example, we must not remove consequences.

When I was a kid, television highlighted parents, especially fathers, who were doing it right. One show we watched on our small black and white screen was "Father Knows Best." It actually began on the radio in 1949, debuted on CBS in October 1954, then was on NBC for three seasons, and then returned to CBS until May 1960. The show highlighted what was then a typical family consisting of a wise father, Jim Anderson who worked outside the home, and his wife Margaret who lovingly cared for him and their children. There was Betty who was boy crazy, Bud who was an all-American boy, and their whiny little sister Kathy. They represented the best of American Families.

The mirror of television has not been kind to fathers since the sixties. Typical husbands and fathers have been represented by Tim the Toolman, Raymond Barone and his obnoxious chauvinist father Frank. Women have been represented by Jill, Deb, and Marie, the overbearing mother of Raymond and Robert.

A closer look at the Prodigal son's Father brings hope and insight.

📖 Then He said: "A certain man had two sons. [12] And the younger of them said to *his* father, 'Father, give me the portion of goods that falls *to me.*' So he divided to them *his* livelihood. Luke 15:11–12.

At first, this looks like a typical family, other than a wife or mother is not mentioned. It is far more difficult when a parent does not have support of the other parent of a prodigal. I cannot determine what happened to the father's spouse. I suspect she may have died prematurely, which would have compounded the problem. I feel for parents of prodigals who do not have loving support from a spouse.

The older son appears to be fairly compliant. He represents the Jews who knew the Law and fulfilled it by their actions, yet only had a form of religion, denying the love and power of God. The younger son kicked against the goads. He represents the Gentiles who did not know the Law. He was free spirited and wanted to do things his way, in his preferred timing. He knew one third share of his father's inheritance would be his. He wanted his share right then! Therefore, his father divided his livelihood to both sons. Two thirds to the oldest son who was responsible for taking care of his parents until they died, and one third to the younger son who was not saddled with the burden of elder care.

The underlying moral of the story is:
The Father's tough love won both sons back.

This Father, representing God The Heavenly Father, loved both sons equally but differently. He provided two portions for the older son to take care of himself, and his parent or parents when they aged. He gave the younger son just one portion, because his only responsibility was to take care of himself.

He failed to do so! There weren't any strings attached to the younger son's portion. It was freely given and became the son's property to use or abuse however he chose. It was a one-time gift, cutting off any access to His father's or brother's remaining wealth.

Father allowed the prodigal to experience
the highs and lows of his foolishness.

📖 And not many days after, the younger son gathered all together, journeyed to a far country, and there wasted his possessions with prodigal living. Luke 15:13.

The prodigal was free to live it up with wine, women, and song. He had a lot of friends because the party crowd flocks around anyone who has money to blow. I'm sure his father continued praying for his lost son, but he knew better than to interfere, but take his hands off so his son could experience consequences of the folly of his ways. He wisely let him experience the highs of prodigal living, knowing there was little likelihood of him coming to his senses until he also experienced the full consequences of ongoing sin and rebellion.

**The wise father did not protect his prodigal
from the just recompense of his foolishness.**

Here is where the story gets really interesting. We see the Father's wisdom in letting his youngest son experience the fullness of his folly. Look at it.

📖 But when he had spent all, there arose a severe famine in that land, and he began to be in want. ¹⁵ Then he went and joined himself to a citizen of that country, and he sent him into his fields to feed swine. ¹⁶ And he would gladly have filled his stomach with the pods that the swine ate, and no one gave him *anything*. Luke 15:14–16.

**The prodigal's father, representing heavenly father,
refused to ease his son's self-induced dilemma.**

While James says pure and undefiled religion is to take care of the widow and the orphan (James 1:27), the prodigal son was neither an orphan nor widowed. He made his own bed and "father knew best" to let him learn his lesson. He did not send his son a care package, pay his chariot payment, or send him a gift package. He understood it takes fullness of godly sorrow to lead to repentance (2 Corinthians 7:10).

One huge danger in the modern do-gooders' mentality of parents and government is their handouts circumvent prodigals from experiencing the wages of their sin, so they never fully experience the consequences of their prodigal ways.

I am going to confess something I've never shared with anyone. When I was a hard-working farm boy, I got so hungry I ate cow food. I loved the clumps in the milk replacer before it was stirred into water for calves. It was better than malted milk mix. The little alfalfa pellets in the feed for calves after they were weaned helped fill my growling stomach. I ate so much wild mustard and alfalfa; it is a wonder I never mooed.

The prodigal son was so hungry he would have gladly eaten the carob pods out of a pig's trough!

Prodigals do not appreciate what they have until they lose it.

📖 A satisfied soul loathes the honeycomb, But to a hungry soul every bitter thing *is* sweet. Proverbs 27:7.

Hunger is a great motivator. That is why Paul wrote,

📖 For even when we were with you, we commanded you this: If anyone will not work, neither shall he eat.
2 Thessalonians 3:10.

The prodigal was willing to work, but given his prodigal lifestyle, all he could swing was a low-responsibility, low-paying job offered to vagrants. Thankfully, the story does get better.

It is doubtful his life would have improved if well-meaning rescuers had given him handouts rather than letting the wages of sin convince him that there is a way that seems right to a man, but the end thereof is destruction (Proverbs 14:12). May God guide us in His ways to truly help prodigals!

The wisdom of refusing the temptation to bail him out.

📖 "But when he came to himself, he said, 'How many of my father's hired servants have bread enough and to spare, and I perish with hunger! [18] I will arise and go to my father, and will say to him, "Father, I have sinned against heaven and before you, [19] and I am no longer worthy to be called your son. Make me like one of your hired servants."' Luke 15:17–19.

This prodigal came to his senses partly because no one entitled his prodigal living.

Admittedly, it is difficult to watch someone you love suffer, even when it is their own fault. It is even harder when there are children involved. But this son needed to experience the wages of his sin in order to come to his senses, humble himself, and become a true servant of God. The Son of Man came to seek and save that which is lost (Luke 19:9–10). But first, they must realize how lost they are before they will turn to God for salvation.

What happened next?
The Father's prayers were finally answered.

Luke 15:20 shows Father did know best. Even though it was painful to hear of his son reaping the consequences of his sin, the best response was to let the boy become as sick of his sin as his father was. The next verse illustrates the Father's great love and compassion moved him to do the hardest thing he could do—let him suffer until . . ..

📖 "And he arose and came to his father. But when he was still a great way off, his father saw him and had compassion, and ran and fell on his neck and kissed him. 21 And the son said to him, 'Father, I have sinned against heaven and in your sight, and am no longer worthy to be called your son.' Luke 15:20–21.

The lesson: Do not intervene until your prodigal fully repents.

It seems evident the prodigal practiced his confession every step of his journey home. I'm not sure whether the father's greatest grace was falling on his boy's neck and kissing him when he finally came home, or not stepping in to rescue his son until he came to his senses.

Let the party begin.

📖 "But the father said to his servants, 'Bring out the best robe and put *it* on him, and put a ring on his hand and sandals on *his* feet. 23 And bring the fatted calf here and kill *it and* let us eat and be merry; 24 for this my son was dead and is alive again; he was lost and is found.' And they began to be merry. Luke 15:22–24.

What a beautiful picture of true salvation and repentance! This represents the heart of Jesus and Abba father who do not begin celebrating until the prodigal is fully home. It reminds me of the words of Jesus to the Pharisees who rebuked Him for reaching out to Zacchaeus and his unsaved friends.

> 📖 And Jesus said to him, "Today salvation has come to this house, because he also is a son of Abraham; [10] for the Son of Man has come to seek and to save that which was lost." Luke 19:9–10.

I met a father who resembled the prodigal's father. His daughter had rebelled in her late teens and ran to a big city where she ended up addicted to cocaine. She sold her body for years to support her habit. She too, finally came to her senses and returned home. She was so demonized her father's pastor suggested he bring her to me. She was a mess. Thin, weak, emotionally unstable. A mere shadow of her previous beauty.

She said demons were screaming from her private places. Had she gone to a hospital she would have been referred to a mental ward. Her father sat in the corner as she confessed her sins, and I broke soul-ties and cast demons out of her. Her Father's love never failed her. He wanted her to receive forgiveness, healing, and deliverance from Jesus. He showed absolutely no embarrassment, shame, or condemnation. His heart's desire was to see her whole. God did a great work in her that day. She went home and continued to grow and heal as she returned home to her parents and their church.

There were two prodigal sons.

Parents sometimes focus so much on the extreme behavior of prodigals, they ignore the less extreme negative behaviors of their "good" children. The second son never left his father. He remained comfortable doing the same old, same old duties but his heart was far from his father and brother. He was not happy his younger brother returned home. He wanted to reject his brother forever: "Goodbye—good riddance!"

📖 "Now his older son was in the field. And as he came and drew near to the house, he heard music and dancing. ²⁶ So he called one of the servants and asked what these things meant. ²⁷ And he said to him, 'Your brother has come, and because he has received him safe and sound, your father has killed the fatted calf.' ²⁸ "But he was angry and would not go in.
Luke 15:25–28a.

The older son stayed at his father's house but strayed from his heart.

The older son, who represented the Jews of Jesus' day, didn't want to have anything to do with his brother when he returned in repentance. He didn't trust him, didn't like him, and was envious when his father celebrated his brother's return while his own good works were ignored. He shared a similar temptation with other siblings in families and churches. He thought he was too good to associate with someone who had really messed up. His father rebuked him.

Prodigals need their entire family to welcome them home.

📖 Therefore his father came out and pleaded with him. ²⁹ So he answered and said to *his* father, 'Lo, these many years I have been serving you; **I never transgressed** your commandment at any time; and yet you never gave me a young goat, that I might make merry with my friends. ³⁰ But as soon as **this son of yours** came, who has devoured your livelihood with harlots, you killed the fatted calf for him.' [31] "And he said to him, 'Son, you are always with me, and all that I have is yours. Luke 15:28b–31.

I don't really believe what the older brother claimed, "I never transgressed your commandment at any time." Do you? Do you believe he had *never* transgressed? Have any of your children *never* transgressed? Have you *never* disobeyed God? We have all sinned and fallen short of the glory of God (Romans 3:23). The religious Jews have, gentiles have, the younger brother had, as did his older brother. I am intrigued by the linguistics of both son and father here.

In verse 30 the older son says, **"this son of yours**." In verse 32 the father says, "**your brother**." This begs the question, who really is responsible for prodigals? Everyone!

📖 [32] It was right that we should make merry and be glad, for **your brother** was dead and is alive again, and was lost and is found.'"

The final lesson here is this: we need the heart of the Father to win prodigals.

Blessing: Heavenly Father is tough when tough is the only thing that will bring prodigals to their senses. He is always compassionate. He knows best: prodigals must be allowed to suffer the consequences of their ways. But He never quits hoping, looking, and waiting for the prodigal to return.

I bless you in the Name of Jesus to be a recipient of and a living expression of God's love, acceptance, and forgiveness. May you have His tough love to let your prodigal suffer until he or she comes to full repentance. May you share His patience, loving acceptance, forgiveness, and the faith needed to know and trust when your prodigal has truly come home. May we, as Christ's body on earth, do His will, His way, until every prodigal is restored. So, help us God!

Take a moment to ask Holy Spirit: "What are you saying to me through this chapter?" Jot down any thoughts He gives you and pray; make them a matter of prayer and meditation.

Prayer: Heavenly Father, You always know best. I confess I certainly don't. I have tried rescuing prodigals before they have experienced the full measure of their sin and it has not worked. I have been tempted to totally give up on some, but I am grateful You have never given up on me. Please give me both Your heart and Your wisdom concerning prodigals. Help me to speak what You are speaking and do what You are doing on their behalf. Help me to want everything You want for them—good or bad. I thank You that Your goodness leads some to repentance. I also thank you for the godly sorrow which leads to repentance. I cry out for wisdom and the courage to do your will, your way, concerning prodigals. In Jesus' Name, amen.

Chapter Six: The Father's Example

We have considered the heavenly meaning of the earthly stories of the Lost Coin, the Lost Sheep, and what I've concluded is an improper title, the Parable of the Lost Son. The real focus is on the prodigal's parent and what he did right, not the son and everything he did wrong. The younger son proved himself incapable of making wise decisions, so his father, representing Heavenly Father, plugged into God's wisdom which helped save his son. A rule of good teaching: to teach you must repeat. The lessons of Luke 15 are repeated in each of its parables.

The Parable of the Lost Coin reveals the need to seek until you find. The Parable of the Lost Sheep demonstrates the heart of the Father seeking to save a single sheep that has strayed from the flock. He left the ninety-nine to seek and save the lost one.

In this chapter we will take a deeper look at the Parable of the Prodigal's Father who represents "Our Father who art in heaven." Let's look.

The prodigal's Father allowed his son to make huge mistakes.

He did not try to micromanage or manipulate and control his son. He realized adult children are free will moral agents to make good or bad choices. Such freedom is wonderful when right choices are made. It steals, kills, and destroys when wrong choices are made. This Father also knew his son would experience the consequences of wrong choices. A tell-tale sign of his greed was his "give me, give me, give me attitude."

📖 Then He said: "A certain man had two sons. ¹²And the younger of them said to *his* father, 'Father, **give me** the portion of goods that falls *to me.*' So he divided to them *his* livelihood. Luke 15:11–12.

The boy thought having riches without working for them would bring prestige. He had a "give me, give me" attitude. The prodigal's father, like our Father in Heaven, wanted his son to do the right thing yet allowed him to make wrong choices and face the consequences.

The prodigal's father let his son mess up and pay the price.

📖 And not many days after, the younger son gathered all together, journeyed to a far country, and there wasted his possessions with prodigal living. ¹⁴But when he had spent all, there arose a severe famine in that land, and **he began to be in want**. Luke 15:13–14.

This story would not have had a happy ending had the father bailed him out, sent him a care package, or helped him get food stamps or disability. Had he sent his boy a healthy allowance, his son would have continued wasting his own, and his father's resources through prodigal living. If Pops had sent him money for rent, car payments, take out or groceries, his son would not have begun being in want.

A major purpose of the Book of Proverbs is helping parents rear godly children according to Words of Wisdom designed to train parents and children to know the mind of Christ and walk in wisdom. WOW—Words Of Wisdom. Proverbs is written to help parents keep their children from going rogue and to win them back if they do!

**If you want to know the mind of God,
read a chapter of Proverbs daily.**

There are thirty-one Proverbs and up to thirty-one days in a month. Perhaps God is trying to tell us something. Several Psalms and Proverbs share the need to recognize the snare of folly:

📖 Every prudent *man* acts with knowledge, But a fool lays open *his* folly. Proverbs 13:16.

We might be tempted to ignore or try to fix a child's folly. We fear they won't love us unless we bail them out, pay their fines, or hire expensive lawyers. Proverbs, however, permits a fool to lay open—for all to see—their folly.

📖 The wisdom of the prudent *is* to understand his way, But the folly of fools *is* deceit. Proverbs 14:8.

Prodigals are experts at deceiving and being deceived. Addicts say they are not addicted and can quit anytime they want. Then why don't they? Do they like wasting their money, destroying their health, looking over their shoulder in fear of being caught in their folly?

📖 The crown of the wise is their riches, *But* the foolishness of fools *is* folly. Proverbs 14:24.

Foolishness means lacking good sense or judgment. It is stupidity. To rob a foolish child of the lessons God wants them to learn only supports his/her foolishness!

📖 Understanding *is* a wellspring of life to him who has it. But **the correction of fools** *is* folly. Proverbs 16:22.

How often do well meaning parents and spouses circumvent God's correction of fools? Losing a job, a place to live, a car, etc. may be exactly what a son or daughter needs to experience so they will come to their senses. The correction of folly is often necessary for prodigals to learn the error of their ways.

Both the mind of God and the heart of God are crucial in restoring prodigals.

An atheist spouts "There is no God." Tell the atheist his name is in the Bible. You can read it right out of the pages of Scripture.

📖 The **fool** has said in his heart, *"There is* no God." They are corrupt, They have done abominable works, There is none who does good. Psalm 14:1; 53:1.

A common trait of prodigals is bragging they do not believe in the Jesus. They "know" a better way than God's! They are wise in their own eyes. They often create false gods or religions to deify their foolish ways.

📖 I will hear what God the LORD will speak, For He will speak peace To His people and to His saints; But let them not turn back to folly. Psalm 85:8.

God does speak peace and wisdom, but only to those who truly follow him.

📖 See a person who is wise in his own eyes? There is more hope for a fool than for him. Proverbs 26:12.

It is never, never, never wise to support a child's foolishness!

As Proverbs reveal the wisdom of God, Psalms reveals His heart.

If you want to know the heart of God, read Psalms each day.

One way to read through Psalms in a month is to follow the calendar date, read that day's Psalm, then add thirty to it five times. For example, on the first day of the month read Psalm 1, 31, 61, 91, and 121. The prodigal's father followed the example of Heavenly Father's wisdom and heart.

The Prodigal's Father did not come to the rescue.

📖 Then he went and joined himself to a citizen of that country, and he sent him into his fields to feed swine. ¹⁶ And he would gladly have filled his stomach with the (carob) pods that the swine ate, and **no one** gave him *anything*. Luke 15:15–16.

We do not like to see our children hurt. We want to help those who most need help. Our instinct is to relieve their suffering. But sometimes we need to give them a hand up rather than a handout. Verse 16 says no one gave him anything. Not his friends, and not his father, and certainly not his brother. No synagogue or welfare agency bailed him out. Such tough love is tough on parents and children, but it accomplished its good work in the prodigal son.

The Prodigal's Father let godly sorrow produce repentance.

📖 For godly sorrow produces repentance *leading* to salvation, not to be regretted; but the sorrow of the world produces death. 2 Corinthians 7:10.

Isn't this what we want for prodigals? What parent does not want God's best for each child? We must never forget—Father knows best. There are times we must step out of God's way!

I do not want to create a greater risk of early death by trying to comfort children when their greater need is to experience godly sorrow. Do you? Many times, it takes getting people we love to reach the bottom of the barrel before they realize their need for change.

I learned the biblical value of spanking when my children were young. I did not understand it, or believe it was helpful when I was spanked with my dad's belt. Oh, that hurt! Yet it probably saved me from drunkenness, drunk driving, crime, and addiction.

Before I continue, let me mention how I understand spanking was designed by God for children, not adults. There comes a time when we must step aside and let God do the spanking.

When my young children were rebellious or disobedient, and did not obey my clear instructions, I took them to an empty room, had them bend over the bed, placed my hand over the bottom of their spine so I wouldn't hurt their back if they wiggled. Then I slowly but firmly spanked them until they began crying in repentance. It is easy to tell when angry rebellious behavior turns to godly sorrow. Such spanking is not abuse. It is parenting as described by the God of the Word in the Word of God.

When a child began crying repentantly, I took them into my arms and loved on them, explained why I had to spank them. Within a few minutes our relationship was restored to better than before.

Some people do not believe in spanking. They are wise in their own eyes and disobey what God tells parents to do throughout the book of Proverbs. Read it and see!

There are nine verses in Proverbs highlighting the value of spanking disobedient children. I will only share one, but you can google the others. If you are really curious, you can look up how God uses the word ROD in 103 verses in the Old Testament and eight verses in the New Testament. Many of them, especially in Proverbs, speak to the wisdom of corporal correction.

📖 The **rod** and rebuke give wisdom, But **a child left** *to himself* **brings shame** to his mother. Proverbs 29:15.

Spanking in love works well with young children through mid-teens. It isn't nearly as practical when our children are bigger and stronger than we are. Still if the rod is applied when they are younger, it is seldom needed when they grow older.

The purpose of discipline is to break a child's stubborn, selfish will. We never want to break a child's spirit, but we must break their will. We break a child's spirit by calling them names and degrading them. "Stupid, idiot, you don't have the brains God gave a goose." "You aren't worth a tinker's damn, etc.," breaks their spirits. Loving children enough to discipline them is what breaks their stubborn wills.

The Prodigal's Father knew when to step back and let God do the spanking and apply His rod of correction.

Praise God! If we step out of the way, He will continue breaking a rebellious adult child's will—if we stay out of the way. When I was 36 years old, God spanked me by letting me roll my brand-new Dodge Charger. He spanked me through infirmity, high insurance, tickets, being thrown off a horse, a house fire, etc. Nobody but God could rescue me. I am grateful no one tried.

Remember, in this Parable the Father represents Heavenly Father who knows best. Unhindered by parents interfering with His loving discipline of the younger son, God disciplined him until he came to his senses. If parents neglect the use of biblical punishment, their children end up facing greater punishment by the Lord! The rod God used on the prodigal son was letting him experience the folly of his way.

God's discipline transformed this son from a rebellious, self-seeking, hedonistic, strong headed, entitled brat destined to trouble and an early death, unto new life for a man eager to change.

That is the godly sorrow which led to repentance. Repentance literally means the change of heart and mind God releases to the hearts of people who respond well to his discipline. This younger son practiced his confession all the way home. He never asked for anything more than a chance to start again on the bottom rung of his father's ladder.

📖 "But **when he came to himself,** he said, 'How many of my father's hired servants have bread enough and to spare, and I perish with hunger! 18 I will arise and go to my father, and will say to him, "Father, I have sinned against heaven and before you, [19] and I am no longer worthy to be called your son. Make me like one of your hired servants.'" Luke 15:17–19.

We must pray for prodigals to come to their senses!

Had the prodigal son's father bailed him out, protected him, sent him money, etc., his younger son would never have come to his senses. He would not have discovered the only thing he could do was repent, change his ways, and return home in humility.

The Prodigal's Father did not rush things to spare his son the just consequences for the folly of his ways. It worked!

📖 "And he arose and came to his father. Luke 15:20a.

When it comes to repentance, each individual must choose to take the first step. We get in their way when we try to make it easier on them.

Can you imagine this boy's fear and trepidation as he approached his father and brother whom he had scorned? He was ruined, penniless, gaunt, smelling like a pig farmer without two quarters for the laundry mat.

He came just as he was without one plea: destitute, in need of a bath, haircut, and manicure. He was ashamed and embarrassed. He knew his only hope was humble repentance in confessing his sin in hopes of receiving underserved grace and mercy from his father.

The Prodigal's Father never quit loving and longing for his son—even after he messed up so bad.

📖 But when he was still a great way off, his father saw him and had compassion, and ran and fell on his neck and kissed him.

(*You can do that once they have started home.*) 21 And the son said to him, 'Father, I have sinned against heaven and in your sight, and am no longer worthy to be called your son.'
Luke 15:20b–21.

The Father's heart never quit looking, hoping, or praying. He tried to still his fears and dared to believe God would somehow redeem his son. Before the prodigal took his share of his father's inheritance and left home to live what he expected to be the dream life, he was proud, wise in his own eyes, and confident in his self-sufficiency.

Understand this: God loves prodigals even more than their parents do. His wisdom is greater than ours and His thoughts higher than our thoughts for our children.

God was working things together for his good the entire time. Apart from a parent's interference — God got the job done!

God worked good through the boy's squandering all his money forever. God used the boy's poverty and destitution for his good. And when the prodigal was fully trained by God's discipline, he was ready to return home and begin a better life.

Celebration takes place after repentance has its full effect.

📖 "But the father said to his servants, 'Bring out the best robe and put *it* on him, and put a ring on his hand and sandals on *his* feet. 23 And bring the fatted calf here and kill *it and* let us eat and be merry; 24 for this my son was dead and is alive again; he was lost and is found.' And they began to be merry.
Luke 15:22–23.

We should not begin celebrating before God has finished his discipline. It is better to celebrate life than death. The prodigal's father knew better than throwing a party when his son was living in rebellion. But he was ready to party hardy when his lost son came home.

There were two prodigal sons, but one stayed home.

📖 "Now his older son was in the field. And as he came and drew near to the house, he heard music and dancing. ²⁶ So he called one of the servants and asked what these things meant. ²⁷ And he said to him, 'Your brother has come, and because he has received him safe and sound, your father has killed the fatted calf.' Luke 15:25–27.

It is obvious to me the older brother's heart wasn't with the Father's any more than his younger brother's had been. Even though he stayed home, he was more concerned for his own prestige and welfare than he was for his brother's salvation.

The older son thought his father should play favorites.

Big brother was angry and antisocial. He refused to join the party and rejoice over his brother's return.

The Father did not gloss over either son's sin.

📖 "But he was angry and would not go in. Therefore his father came out and pleaded with him. ²⁹ So he answered and said to *his* father, 'Lo, these many years I have been serving you; I never transgressed your commandment at any time; and yet you never gave me a young goat, that I might make merry with my friends. ³⁰ But as soon as this son of yours came, who has devoured your livelihood with harlots, you killed the fatted calf for him.' Luke 15:28–30.

Consider the older son's verbiage. He said to his father: **"This son of YOURS."** Big brat brother tried pulling the splinter out of his little brother's eye and his father's eye before removing the log from his own eye. He didn't want anything to do with his younger sibling. Tell me, do you think the older brother never transgressed his father's commandment at any time? I think most children think their siblings' faults are greater than their own. Parents often have to deal with the scourge of judgmental attitudes from their "good" children concerning their prodigals.

The older brother refused to acknowledge any personal responsibility for his brother and His father refused to release him from responsibility for his sibling.

Let's face the facts: the older brother had an inflated ego, was full of anger and pride, and critical of both his father and brother. He was bent out of shape because he was envious because his father joyfully celebrated the homecoming of his brother.

The Father rejoiced at his younger son's homecoming but did not restore his loss.

📖 "And he said to him, 'Son, you are always with me, and **all that I have is yours**. ³² It was right that we should make merry and be glad, for **your brother** was dead and is alive again, and was lost and is found.'" Luke 15:31–32.

It is painful when someone's child writes off a brother or sister. You see it all the time. Children are critical of their siblings and their parents. Notice the Father's verbiage, "YOUR brother." He was holding the older brother responsible for his younger brother. At the same time, this wise father resisted the temptation to fix everything his prodigal messed up.

The Father did not replace what the prodigal wasted.

The younger boy had squandered his inheritance. Zilch, gone, lost forever. Such is part of Heavenly Father's justice. As the boy sowed, so shall he reap (Galatians 6:7).

The Father rejoiced over what God rejoices over.

📖 I say to you that likewise there will be more joy in heaven over **one sinner** who **repents** than over ninety-nine just persons who need no repentance. Luke 15:7.

Nothing is better than seeing a sinner repent and surrender fully to the Lord! If any prodigal is in Christ, he or she is a new creature, the old is gone and the new is come (2 Corinthians 5:17).

In the next chapter, we will begin looking at specific strategies for helping wayward children come to the point where they can be saved and transformed.

Take a moment to ask Holy Spirit: "What are you saying to me through this chapter?" Jot down any thoughts He gives you and pray; make them a matter of prayer and meditation.

Prayer: Heavenly Father, please give me enough faith to do Your will, Your way, concerning prodigals. Teach me the distinction between helping and enabling. Give me guidance in how to guide "runaway" prodigals as well as those who refuse to leave the nest. Let me know everything You want me to do and when and how to do it. I also ask Your guidance in when it is best to withhold support. Today I decree: Heavenly Father knows best, and He will guide me concerning prodigals. In Jesus' Name.

Chapter Seven: Satan's Schemes

I cannot think of anything I have written that has taken more God and guts than *Parents & Prodigals*. This chapter is no exception. Here we turn to some spiritual aspects of prodigals and those who love them. This may take some time to unfold. We need to recognize the enemy, then develop and engage strategies to defeat him.

📖 The thief does not come **except** to steal, and to kill, and to destroy. I have come that they may have life, and that they may have *it* more abundantly. John 10:10.

Satan does not come to our descendants EXCEPT to steal, kill, and destroy God's prodigals and the prodigals of the world. He wants to destroy every prodigal, plus you and me. He uses sin, temptation, media, WOKE, Critical Race Theory, gender confusion, gaming, pornography, leftist politics, promiscuity, addiction, and crime to steal, kill, and destroy.

Jesus came so we (and our descendants) might have life and have it MORE abundantly. Soon we see how the enemy uses wayward inheritance and patterns of perversity to steal, kill, and destroy our children.

The Devil is bent on destroying every child of destiny.

We must take heed! Thankfully, God has a perfect blueprint for every life. Satan, however, has programming, including some from their ancestors, to throw every child of God off track. Let me share some examples.

Satan wanted to steal, kill, and destroy Moses. In Exodus Chapter 1, the devil did not care how many male babies the midwives killed, he just wanted to make sure God's destined deliverer, Moses, would not be allowed to live (Exodus 1:16) Note: Satan's plans were spoiled. Hallelujah!

Satan wanted to steal, kill, and destroy the One destined to be King of the Jews, and he did not care how many boys under the age of two were murdered to get to Jesus. He used King Herod's fear of a child destined to be a King, to move him to send forth and put to death all the male children who were in Bethlehem and in all its districts, from two years old and under (Matthew 2:16). Note: Satan's plans were spoiled. Hallelujah!

Another case, more difficult to understand, comes from history in Revelation.

And another sign appeared in heaven: behold, a great, fiery red dragon having seven heads and ten horns, and seven diadems on his heads. ⁴ His tail drew a third of the stars of heaven and threw them to the earth. And the dragon stood before the woman who was ready to give birth, to devour her Child as soon as it was born. ⁵ She bore a male Child who was to rule all nations with a rod of iron. And her Child was caught up to God and His throne. ⁶ Then the woman fled into the wilderness, where she has a place prepared by God, that they should feed her there one thousand two hundred and sixty days. Revelation 12:3–6.

The woman represents God's chosen nation of Israel and is described as giving birth to a "male Child who was to rule all nations with a rod of iron" (Revelation 12:5).

The language here makes it clear Jesus is the "Child" in Revelation 12. The great dragon is the serpent of old, called the Devil and Satan, who deceives the whole world. Note: Satan's plans were spoiled. Hallelujah!

The Devil is bent on destroying every child of destiny And every ancestor of children of destiny.

Psalm 139, Jeremiah 1:7, 29:11–12, and Ephesians 4:10 say every child—including every adult child is formed on purpose. God has great thoughts for every child. Jeremiah states God knows and appoints every person at birth. He later states He knows the plans He has to prosper and not harm every person. Ephesians Chapter 4 speaks of the prophetic destiny God has for every life. Satan wants to spoil God's plans.

If Satan can get the ancestors of a child of destiny, he will have an opening to steal, kill, and destroy their children and grandchildren—unless we intervene!

📖 Thus says the Lord: "A voice was heard in Ramah, Lamentation *and* bitter weeping, Rachel weeping for her children, Refusing to be comforted for her children, Because they *are* no more." Jerimiah 31:15

I explain how the Midianite curse works in my book, *Busting Through to Greater Freedom*.[1] Satan's schematics working through the spirits controlling the Canaanite tribes are still active, as are the spirits that take advantage of ancestral sin as well as personal sin.

Midianite preys on people when they or their ancestors have chosen comfort over calling. Gideon's tribe, for example, chose to backdown from battle rather than face their enemies and conquer them. Gideon tried hiding in a wine vat beating out the grain, before answering God's call to go to battle.

Satan wanted to steal, kill, and destroy Rachel and her children. Sadly, Rachel died in childbirth, so her children were "no more to her." In deliverance ministry we often cast out Rachel Spirits from parents of aborted children and/or other children who died before their time. Perhaps we need to bind the Rachel spirit from parents who are weeping for their wayward children who, in the present, "are no more?"

On January 1, 1974, James Arthur Vauss published his life story, *The devil loves a shining mark.*[2] I read it as a young Christian. Vauss had been in the mob and shared how the devil tried to destroy him before he was saved. Michael J. Lindell, the "pillow guy," shares a similar story. Note: Satan's plans were spoiled for both these "shining marks." Hallelujah!

The devil is out to destroy the image of God in people, and he won't stop short of killing them, if he can do so. We must stand, and having done all, continue to stand on their behalf. The devil, the destroyer of life, was behind the 30,074 abortions in my home State of Michigan in 2021. He is working through the perverted liberal mindsets making abortion easily assessable even after Row vs. Wade was overturned. Why? Satan does not come

except to steal, and to kill, and to destroy. Satan is after our children!

Catch this: the Devil is bent on destroying children because of their prophetic destinies. The higher their destiny, the more aggressive Satan is in his attempt to steal, kill and destroy. Are you catching who is trying to destroy every prodigal? Satan, the devil, that great dragon of old who had always tried to devour people with a destiny! It is time to fight this battle God's way. Note: We must fight until Satan's plans are spoiled. Hallelujah!

We must determine to expose and destroy Satan's programming for Prodigals and pray them into the fulness of God's blueprint for their lives.

My goal in this book is not to sell more books, but to point to revelation to help in the battle for prodigals. In 2014, I was strongly led to write a book to counteract the unscriptural thinking that "whatever will be, will be" and God alone determines the destiny of every person.

I wrote the 183-page book *Schematics God's Blueprint versus Satan's Programming*[3] to help people understand how both God's schematics are designed to bring out His best in every person. Satan's schemes to circumvent God's schematics and replace them with schemes of his own. God gives each person freedom to choose His ways or default to the devil's.

Satan has several plots against prodigals.

For though we walk in the flesh, we do not war according to the flesh. [4] For the weapons of our warfare *are* not carnal but mighty in God for pulling down strongholds, [5] casting down

arguments and every high thing that exalts itself against the knowledge of God, bringing every thought into captivity to the obedience of Christ, ⁶ and being ready to punish all disobedience when your obedience is fulfilled.
2 Corinthians 10:3–6.

The word "carnal" used above means "Of the flesh, or soulish." We will take a deeper look at these weapons as we press ahead in a later chapter.

Only as we resist Satan and His ways and choose to partner with Jesus and His ways, can we hope to rescue our own prodigals and other prodigals.

📖 Therefore submit to God. Resist the devil and he will flee from you. *(If you do not resist—the devil will not flee—from you or your children!)* ⁸ Draw near to God and He will draw near to you. Cleanse *your* hands, *you* sinners; and purify your hearts, *you* double-minded. James 4:7–8.

Desperation Band's, *"Counting on God,"* reveals our fight against the powers of darkness. Consider the first verse.

I'm in a fight not physical
And I'm in a war
But not with this world
You are the light that's beautiful
And I want more
I want all that's Yours⁴

As we make this fight about God and His will for us and our prodigals, we will be on the path to victory, but there are some major steps we must take. I struggled with this message for hours before I grasped the meaning of GRACE. Grace is the God-given desire and power to do God's will, God's way, which brings God-sized results! We need exorbitant grace to win the battle for prodigals. I pray release of God's grace as we move onto the next chapter.

Take a moment to ask Holy Spirit: "What are you saying to me through this chapter?" Jot down any thoughts He gives you and pray; make them a matter of prayer and meditation.

Prayer: Heavenly Father, you have wonderful plans for every person. Your arch enemy, the devil hates people because you want to bless them and use them to advance Your Kingdom. Help me seek first Your Kingdom and righteousness for myself and then for the prodigals I care for. Teach me to fight the good fight on their behalf and my own. Give me clarity concerning Your blueprints for those I am praying for. Teach me how to spoil the enemy's plans to destroy them. In Jesus' Powerful Name, amen.

Footnotes:

[1] Douglas E. Carr, *Busting Through to Greater Freedom*. KDP 2017.

[2] James Arthur Vauss, *The Devil Loves a Shining Mark.* Word Books edition, in English *(1974 edition)* January 1, 1974,

[3] Dr. Douglas Carr, *Schematics God's Blueprint versus Satan's Programming.* Create Space, 2014.

[4] Desperation Band *"Counting on God" Verse one.*

Chapter Eight: Judging and Bitterness

Derek Prince wrote the wonderful book *Judging, When, Why, How?* in 2001. It has an Alternative Title: *Sound Judgement.*[1] I read it years ago, but I was greatly impacted by it. If I remember correctly, the main thesis was we have the right to judge those we are responsible for. Since we are responsible for ourselves and our young children, we have both the right and responsibility to make judgments concerning them. We do not have a right to judge another parent's children.

Jesus warned of serious consequences of wrong judging. The words "judge" and" Judgment" used in the following passage can mean "condemn" and "condemnation."

"Judge not, that you be not judged. [2] For with what judgment you judge, **you will be judged**; and with the measure you use, **it will be measured back to you**. [3] And why do you look at the speck in your brother's eye, but do not consider the plank in your own eye? [4] Or how can you say to your brother, 'Let me remove the speck from your eye'; and look, a plank *is* in your own eye? [5] Hypocrite! First remove the plank from your own eye, and then you will see clearly to remove the speck from your brother's eye. Matthew 7:1–5.

We cannot remove the speck in a prodigal's eyes until we address every log in our own eyes.

If the present concern is with a prodigal in one's own child, whether adult or child, it might help if we replace the words "brother's eye" with "child's eye" here. We must deal with personal sin, iniquity, and faults before we have much hope in rescuing our descendants. The first thing that comes to mind is unforgiveness. To be effective in rescuing people we love from bitterness and wrath, we first must be rescued of the same!

We must deal with personal judgments and bitterness if we want to be effective.

Parents and prodigals must forgive each other. We have seen several miraculous healings when people have forgiven those who hurt them most. Often it is a parent or teacher who hurt them when they were young, or a spouse, pastor, or other Believer who hurt them when they were older. Choosing not to forgive gives the devil legal permission to steal, kill, and destroy. The word translated "Place" in verse 27 is often translated "foothold." Look at it.

📖 25 Therefore, putting away lying, "*Let* each one *of you* speak truth with his neighbor," for we are members of one another. 26 "Be **angry**, and do not sin": do not let the sun go down on your **wrath**, 27 nor give **place** to the devil. 28 Let him who stole steal no longer, but rather let him labor, working with *his* hands what is good, that he may have something to give him who has need. 29 Let no corrupt word proceed out of your mouth, but what is good for necessary edification, that it may impart grace to the hearers. Ephesians 4:25–29.

The translated "place" in verse 27 above means giving an opportunity to the devil. It comes from the Greek word "topos." It is the word topography comes from. If someone allows anger or wrath to continue, it gives the devil a literal place, hence opportunity, to stand in our lives.

The first instantaneous miracle I ever witnessed was a woman in her seventies who was instantly healed of crippling arthritis when she chose to forgive her mother for not protecting her from her stepfather when she was a girl. She kept her healing even as she passed from death to life years later. The healing had been blocked until she forgave a longstanding offence.

Lack of forgiveness blocks miraculous healing and family restoration!

Consider the McCoy/Hatfield feud.[2] In 1878 Randolph McCoy accused Floyd Hatfield, a cousin of Devil Anse, of stealing one of his pigs. Rather than experience the grace of forgiveness, this feud continued until many were robbed, killed, and destroyed. The devil wants to rob, kill, and destroy families and churches. He uses bitterness to steal, kill, and destroy us all to keep God's glory from manifesting on the earth. Is that what we want? We must seek God's grace of forgiveness if we want to break Satan's schematic to blow anger to wrath and bitterness into feuding!

Marriages are healed when forgiveness is given and received. Parent-child, preacher-parishioner relationships can be healed through forgiveness. It is no wonder the Lord's Prayer includes the phrase "forgive us our sins as we forgive those who have sinned against us." All have sinned and fallen short of the glory of God (Romans 3:23). That means we have! So, we must receive and release forgiveness. Amen? We have seen instantaneous miracles of healing: diabetes, a shoulder painfully locked by arthritis, and blood sugar instantly lowered from over 200 to 150 through forgiveness.

Take a moment to ask Holy Spirit: "What are you saying to me through this chapter?" Jot down any thoughts He gives you and pray; make them a matter of prayer and meditation.

Take another moment and ask Holy Spirit to reveal any unforgiveness you hold toward your parents, spouse, children, or others.

Bowl of Forgiveness.

During ministry I ask people to make a bowl by cupping their hands together. I have them verbally place in the bowl the people who have hurt them the most and how specific offenses made them feel. I usually take notes so I can lead them through prayer of forgiving. Before I ask them to forgive, however, I ask them how heavy the bowl is. Common answers are "really heavy," "so heavy I cannot hold it up for long," etc. Then I ask them to picture or imagine Jesus in the room with us. (Jesus manifests His presence in special ways when two or three are gathered together.) Once they can picture Him, I ask them to forgive the people for what they did and for how it made them feel. Once they finish, I encourage them to hand the bowl to Jesus, and then I ask them, "What did Jesus do with the bowl?" They often report He throws it into a fire, over His shoulder, stomps on it, or it simply disappears. Interestingly, when doing this in group settings, people often see Jesus doing exactly the same thing with their bowls.

Prayer: Jesus, You taught us to ask The Father to forgive us **as** we forgive those who sin against us. Hebrews 12:14–15 warns us to be careful lest we fall short of the grace of God through any root of bitterness. Today, I examine my own heart in order to recognize and take care of any personal roots of bitterness.

I choose to be honest with myself and you about what the prodigals in my life have done to hurt me and how they have made me feel. (Jot notes down if it will help.)

I choose to forgive those who hurt me, and I choose to forgive myself. I offer You my pain and sorrow.

My prayer for you:

Father, I pray for every person who has been hurt by the behaviors of prodigals whom they love. I ask You to comfort parents who are morning over their prodigals, whether living or dead. Please give strength, comfort, insight, and great grace. In Jesus' Name, Amen.

Endnotes:

[1] Derek Prince, *Judging, When, Why, How?* in 2001. It has an Alternative Title: *Sound Judgement.*[1] Available new and used from many sites on the web, including Derek Prince Ministries. [2] McCoy/Hatfield feud. My words are based on various sources and oral traditions.

Chapter Nine: Iniquitous Patterns of Perversity

📖 And God spoke all these words, saying: ² "I *am* the Lord your God, who brought you out of the land of Egypt, out of the house of bondage. Exodus 20:1–2.

Bondage speaks of being slaves to evil rulers whether human or spiritual. Egypt represents the kingdom of darkness; Pharoah represents Satan, the devil is also called "that ancient red fiery dragon." Slavery in Scripture can also refer to being slaves to sin. When people fail to resist darkness and bondage, they are taken captive. This is true for us and our descendants.

In Exodus 20:3–5, God expresses the danger of idolatry in any form.

📖 "You shall have no other gods before Me. ⁴ "You shall not make for yourself a carved image—any likeness *of anything* that *is* in heaven above, or that *is* in the earth beneath, or that *is* in the water under the earth; ⁵ you shall not bow down to them nor serve them. Exodus 20:3-5. (The word for "serve" can mean worship.)

God gave a stern warning about idolatry at the beginning of the Ten Commandments. The word "Idolatry" in the New Testament comes from two Greek Words, "Idwn" which means to see, and "Latria" which means to worship. Whenever we, or our children, worship things visible rather than our invisible God, it is idolatry. Even churches can become idolatrous when they put programing and lust for growth before pure undefiled religion of taking care of widows and orphans (James 1:27). Putting school, career, sports, or material things before God is idolatry.

Pastors see parents putting their children's sports before attending church. If there is a ball game, dance recital, fishing tournament, etc. that interferes with church activities, parents often prioritize the sports before faithful attendance in church. Then they wonder why their children do not think church is important when they leave home.

Some churches teach people to worship idols and icons, and even to pray to them. Many lodges and secret societies, fraternities, and sororities are idolatrous. The next passage is the Bible's third mention of iniquity. The consequences of idolatry are listed here. Idolatry gives Satan legal right to steal, kill, and destroy, not only the guilty but their ancestors.

📖 For I, the Lord your God, *am* a jealous God, visiting *(punishing)* the *iniquity* of the fathers upon the children to the third and fourth *generations* of those who hate Me, ⁶but showing mercy to thousands, to those who love Me and keep My commandments. Exodus 20:5b–6.

Jesus said those who obey Him, love Him. Those who hate Him, disobey Him. One curse and iniquitous pattern that is often passed down generationally is the curse of neglecting the things of God, along with the iniquitous pattern of a take it or leave it attitude toward worship and honoring the Lord.

Though God tells men to be the first line of defense in homes and families, iniquities often get in the way. Some homes and generations have few if any godly men. Iniquitous patterns of fathers *and* mothers will be visited upon the children for at least three or four generations. We often observe iniquitous patterns coming through one or both parent's ancestral lines.

Unless dealt with, descendants own their ancestors' iniquities.

Thankfully, parents of prodigals can address iniquitous patterns from their ancestors and descendants. Since only eight of the sixty-four translations I used in this study rightly translate the Hebrew word for "iniquity," I risk boring you with some definitions from Strong's Concordance.

Strongs Hebrew Concordance. Hebrew 5771[1]
   avon: iniquity, guilt, punishment for iniquity
   Original Word: עָוֹן
   Part of Speech: Noun Masculine
   Transliteration: avon
   Phonetic Spelling: (aw-vone')
   Definition: iniquity, guilt, punishment for iniquity

Iniquity can be defined as a bent, twisting, or distortion of character that passes down ancestral lines. My book on this subject is *Patterns of Perversity! Freedom from Iniquity*[2]. A licensed family counselor whom I highly respect uses this book in her family practice and reports good results as she helps people break free of generational patterns of perversity. Iniquities are patterns of perversity flowing through natural, adopted, and stepfamily lines.

A few examples of iniquity are bad temper, obesity, bitterness, selfishness, stinginess, addiction, immorality, entitlement, abuse, victimization, manipulation and control, forms of religion that deny the power of God, and many more. This is so important I offered free copies of *Patterns of Perversity* to members of our congregation. I am convinced books like these will not help if they are left on a table or in a bookshelf. They must be read and put into practice.

Anything worth doing must be done!

It is not enough to be hearers of the word. We must hear them, apply them, and pray them through until we rescue every prodigal. Are their souls worth enough for us to make the effort?

📖 Is any sick among you? let him call for the elders of the church; and let them pray over him, anointing him with oil in the name of the Lord. James 5:14.

Sickness may be physical, mental, emotional, relational, moral, and/or spiritual. Each of these, when flowing through iniquitous patterns should be first addressed at their point of entrance, which is often ancestral.

A Greek word with a similar meaning to iniquity is found in James 5:15. I will give it to you within the larger context.

📖 And the prayer of faith shall save the sick, and the Lord shall raise him up; and if he have committed **sins**, they shall be forgiven him. James 5:15.

Sins, in James 5:15, comes from the Greek word "harmartano" which means missing the mark or God's bullseye for one's life. Let me briefly address this word.

Strongs Greek #266[3]
Word: armartia
Pronounce: ham-ar-tt'-ah.
Orig: from 264; a sin (properly abstract):--offense, sin, sinful. G264.
Use: TDNT-1:267, 44 Noun Feminine H8441
1) equivalent to G264.
1a) to be without a share in
1b) to miss the mark
1c) to err, miss the mark
1d) to miss or wander from the path of uprightness and honour, to do or go wrong.
1e) to wonder from the law of God, violate God's law, sin.
2) that which is done wrong, sin, an offence, a violation of the divine law in thought or in act.
3) collectively, the complex or aggregate of sins committed either by a single person or by many.[3]

HELPS Word-studies:
Usage: originally: I miss the mark, hence (a) I make a mistake, (b) I sin, commit a sin (against God); sometimes the idea of sinning against a fellow-creature is present.[4]

People do sin and miss the mark of God's blueprint for their lives. Unfortunately, their descendants are prone to missing the same or similar marks.

What parents do in moderation,
Their children often do in excess.

Parents who moderately consume alcohol or use drugs stack the odds of having children or grandchildren who do so in excess. James takes us deeper still. There is something much deeper than missing the mark that leads people astray. The Bible translations I prefer use the word "Faults" in James 5:16 though many other translations use "sins." After several hours of study, this left me tired and a bit confused. I use the free version of BibleGateway.com: A searchable online Bible in over 150 versions and 50 languages. I read James 5:16 in 64 versions.

Twelve of them used the words "faults," three used "offenses," and two used "trespasses." The rest of them used sins, wrong things, trespasses, etc. Together, they reveal thus:

God's intent in James 5:16 goes deeper and far beyond specific sins we have personally committed such as lying, stealing, cheating, promiscuity, drinking, smoking, or doing drugs.

God wants us to dig beneath the surface to the underlying
sin nature inherited from Adam in a generic sense
and from direct ancestors in specific ways.

It took me nearly three hours of studying the etymology of the word "faults" used in many translations of James 5:16 before I realized God wanted to show me something else before we finish this point.

We cannot remove the speck in a child's eyes until we deal with every log in our own eyes. Consider James 5:16 from two popular translations.

📖 Confess your **faults** one to another, and pray one for another, that ye may be healed. The effectual fervent prayer of a righteous man availeth much. James 5:16 KJV.

📖 Therefore confess your **sins** to each other and pray for each other so that you may be healed. The prayer of a righteous person is powerful and effective. James 5:16 NIV.

There is a Cause and a Cure for Ancestral Iniquity.

Here we begin examining some openings Satan takes advantage of, to come after us and our children. He seems to delight in using ancestral iniquities against people and their children.

Sins are things we do wrong that offend God. Iniquities are inherited from ancestors who did wrong and offended God.

Unfortunately, it is difficult to study the words "iniquity" and "iniquities" because of their vastly different translations. The majority of modern translations wrongly translate the Hebrew word for iniquity as "sins," and the Greek word best translated as "faults" is incorrectly translated as sins. There are 229 references to iniquity and 52 references to the word "Iniquities" in the New King James Bible.

Sometimes illustrations bring greater understanding and revelation of how iniquities and/or moral excellence impact following generations. There is a well-known case study of Jonathan Edwards and Max Jukes that illustrate this point. It demonstrates how ancestral goodness and/or iniquities often visit subsequent generations.

Two Fathers, Two Families, Two Fates

Jonathan Edwards, one of the greatest minds that God has given America, lived in the state of New York. He was a Christian and believed in Christian training. He married a girl of like character. From this union, men have studied 729 descendants. Of this number came 300 preachers, 65 college professors, 13 university presidents, 60 authors of good books, 3 United States congressmen, and one vice president of the United States. Barring one grandson who married a questionable character, the family has not cost the state a single dollar.

Max Jukes lived in the same state. He did not believe in Christian training. He married a girl of like character. From this union, men have studied 1,026 descendants. Three hundred of them died prematurely, one hundred were sent to the penitentiary for an average of 13 years each, one hundred and ninety were public prostitutes, and one hundred were drunkards. The family cost the state $1,200,000 and they made no helpful contribution to society.

The difference in these two fathers, two families, and two fates was caused by Christian home training and heart conversion, or lack thereof. What choices will you make? What direction will you set for your family? Life is not a bed of roses. However, you may choose to go with God, or you may choose to go alone. Trust the Lord and He will go with you. Yes, the storms of life will come, and the critics will have their opinions, but the Lord will never leave or forsake you.[5]

It is my prayer, each person who hears this message will make an intentional effort to identify iniquitous patterns in their ancestors, themselves, and their descendants. Confessing and renouncing iniquities is a huge step in breaking their power over themselves, their children, and grandchildren.

Take a moment to ask Holy Spirit: "What are you saying to me through this chapter?" Jot down any thoughts He gives you and pray; make them a matter of prayer and meditation.

Prayer: Father, I thank You for sending the Holy Spirit to teach me and remind me of everything He has said and is saying to me. I ask you to lead me in recognizing every iniquitous pattern flowing through the ancestral lines of the prodigals I am concerned for. Reveal specific iniquities and teach me to address them through confession, renouncing, and breaking each one through prayers of faith. In Jesus' Name.

Endnotes:

[1] Strongs Hebrew Concordance. Hebrew 5771.

[2] Dr. Douglas E. Carr, *Breaking Patterns of Perversity Freedom from Iniquity.* 2022, KDP.

[3] Strongs Greek Concordance. Greek 266.

[4] Helps Word Studies, https://go.discoverybible.com/wp-content/uploads/2021/11/G25_to-love.pdf

[5] thevoiceinthewilderness.org *Jonathan Edwards vs Max Jukes.*

Chapter Ten: Crucial Steps before Spiritual Warfare

It felt like a heat wave on March 1st when the thermometer reached 52 degrees. As I drove forty minutes to counsel inmates, I saw a teenager with a short sleeve shirt, shorts, and sandals riding a bike. Even though it was unseasonably warm, he wasn't adequately dressed. Such is the folly of youth. I used to get strep throat every spring because I began riding my little Honda 90 to school and work, without appropriate leathers to break the cold wind. We do not want to jump the gun when engaging in spiritual warfare for prodigals.

People usually grow in common sense as they grow older. The problem with common sense is it isn't very common—ask any parent of a prodigal. One of my Spring Arbor college professors said, "Common sense is just horse sense, and horse sense is good stable thinking." Apart from the counsel of the Lord, we fall short of both. My wife, Pam, made a commonsense comment about prodigals.

God is our Father; sometimes we are His prodigals.

God does not want us to be prodigals any more than we want our children to be. We must confess and repent of all known sin, wrong attitudes, bitterness, etc. before we can be effective in warfare.

We must prepare ourselves before engaging in spiritual warfare for prodigals! When prodigals are held captive by the devil, counseling will not get the job done unless it engages the spiritual components of binding, loosing, and casting out demons, Tranquilizers and psychotropics may lessen symptoms but will not set the captive free. Apart from Holy Spirit unction, counseling and treatments may only deaden the pain and perhaps lessen the exacerbation of things. They may or may not bring healing.

Luke 15 begins with parables of the lost sheep, the lost coin, and ends with the parable of the prodigal son. We have already seen how the prodigal son's father represents Heavenly Father—who never stops loving His children and/or disciplining them out of His loving heart.

The parable of the lost sheep is given four verses in Luke 15:4-7. In Matthew 18, the lost sheep parable is five verses long. God revealed something in the fact the lost sheep is sandwiched in the middle of five major (though be it be man-made) headings in bold print. Their order reveals rescuing prodigals takes more than praying they come to their senses.

Take note of the headings in Matthew 18:

Who is the Greatest? Matthew 18:1–5.

Nobody wins when parents and prodigals jockey for position or importance. A two-year-old can be more emphatic than his or her parents in trying to establish who is in charge. Jesus' solution in this situation says, "Therefore, whoever humbles himself as this little child is the greatest in the kingdom of heaven" (Matthew 18:4). There is a kairos (opportune) time to discipline wayward children, especially when they are young. We can't give up even if we have missed the best time. Their souls are at stake.

There is also a time we need to humbly put ourselves in the prodigal's shoes and try to understand what he or she is walking through.

Jesus Warns of Offenses. Matthew 18:6–9.

We have all sinned and fallen short of the glory of God (Romans 3:23). Accordingly, the majority of parents offend their children one way or another. The first two verses in this section give a solemn warning.

> "But whoever causes one of these little ones who believe in Me to sin, it would be better for him if a millstone were hung around his neck, and he were drowned in the depth of the sea. Matthew 7 Woe to the world because of offenses! For offenses must come, but woe to that man by whom the offense comes! Matthew 18:6-7.

> **The biggest problem we have with children is: they are sinners in need of grace.**

> **The biggest problem prodigals have with us is: we are sinners in need of grace.**

We need to take the plank out of our own eyes before we can remove the speck from a prodigal's eyes. There comes a time we must ask ourselves and Holy Spirit, "What have I done or failed to do that has contributed to a prodigal's wandering?"

Sometimes we may need to ask this question concerning ourselves and a child's other parent.

I think of a senior woman who was miraculously healed after finally forgiving her mother for not protecting her from her stepfather. The stepfather was wrong for abusing her when she was young. But in the girl's heart the greater offense was her mother's failure to protect her. Such things are difficult to address, yet we will IF we are committed to bringing prodigals home. Will we pay the price?

Ask yourself: "Where have I caused my child to sin?" Confess your sin to the Lord and receive His forgiveness. Then confess it to your child and pray he/she will forgive you. This may be key in restoring relationship with prodigals.

📖 "If **your** hand or foot causes you to sin, cut it off and cast *it* from you. It is better for **you** to enter into life lame or maimed, rather than having two hands or two feet, to be cast into the everlasting fire. [9] And if **your** eye causes you to sin, pluck it out and cast *it* from you. It is better for **you** to enter into life with one eye, rather than having two eyes, to be cast into [hell] fire. Matthew 18:8–9.

We do not want to take this to an extreme like some religions do and cut off body parts or gauge eyes out when prodigals touch or look at the wrong things. But verses 8 and 9 stress the importance of cutting things out of our lives that bring sure damnation. Let me include some key Scriptures here to emphasize the need to walking in Biblical conviction. Each of these verses stress our choices have eternal consequences.

I use these passages frequently during ministry. I call the first one "The O Crap" list because many of us have done some of the things listed.

📖 Do you not know that the unrighteous will not inherit the kingdom of God? Do not be deceived. Neither fornicators, nor idolaters, nor adulterers, nor homosexuals, nor sodomites, nor thieves, nor covetous, nor drunkards, nor revilers, nor extortioners will inherit the kingdom of God.
1 Corinthians 6:9–10.

Apart from salvation, the above activities would exclude people from the Kingdom of God. The follow verse describes God's cure and our hope.

📖 And such were some of you. But you were washed, but you were sanctified, but you were justified in the name of the Lord Jesus and by the Spirit of our God. 1 Corinthians 6:11.

I love how the word "were" is used four times in the previous verse, showing the power of the Gospel of Jesus Christ to change our trajectory from hell to heaven, and from the captivity of sin to the power of God's cleansing to personal victory.

Galatians contrasts the captivity of sin to the freedom of spiritual life.

📖 Now the works of the flesh are evident, which are: adultery, [e]fornication, uncleanness, lewdness, idolatry, sorcery, hatred, contentions, jealousies, outbursts of wrath, selfish ambitions, dissensions, heresies, envy, murders, drunkenness, revelries, and the like; of which I tell you beforehand, just as I also told you in time past, that those who practice such things will not inherit the kingdom of God But the fruit of the Spirit is love, joy, peace, longsuffering, kindness, goodness, faithfulness, gentleness, self-control. Against such there is no law. Galatians 5:19–23.

Make no mistake, Jesus came to set us free from the law of sin and death (Romans 8:2), but we face certain judgment if we cannot testify with 1 Corinthians 6:11, we have been washed and cleansed from the old life and freed to walk in love, life, and purity. Consider what Apostle John recorded in Revelation.

📖 But the cowardly, unbelieving, abominable, murderers, sexually immoral, sorcerers, idolaters, and all liars shall have their part in the lake which burns with fire and brimstone, which is the second death." Revelation 21:8.

The Parable of the Lost Sheep. Matthew 18:10–14.

Matthew begins the Parable of the Lost Sheep by waving a caution flag. The devil sees to it that parents are given plenty of reasons to despise their children and vice versa. Jesus says take heed! Satan wants to stir up such hatred that we despise one another! He uses disrespect, selfishness, rebellion, hatred, name calling and the like.

Perhaps this is why Jesus gives such a stern warning. He only mentions the Parable of the Lost Sheep in Matthew 18 but adds an essential warning to it not found in the same parable in Luke 15:4–7.

📖 "**Take heed** that **you do not despise** one of these little ones, for I say to you that in heaven their angels always see the face of My Father who is in heaven. [11] For the Son of Man has come to save that which was lost. Matthew 18:10–11.

Some angels are assigned to children to be heaven's tattletales. They report to Jehovah how we treat others, especially children. I've heard parents and children scream, "I hate you." To this Jesus says, "Take heed, you are missing the heart of the Son of Man."

You cannot reach a prodigal's heart unless your heart is right before them.

Some children carry the hurtful words of their parents for decades. They remember when a parent screamed, "I hate you, I wish you had never been born." Even kind words spoken with sarcasm cut to-the-bone. Many grownups remember specific hurtful words spoken when they were children as if they were spoken yesterday.

We use a questionnaire for people who desire appointments. There is a place to list all sorts of negative words. One question asks, "What are some of the hurtful things or names people have spoken to you?" Many of the hurtful things listed come from one or both parents. Children can easily tell when our hearts are not right toward them, even as parents can tell when a child's heart is not right toward them.

Ask Holy Spirit to reveal ways you have come to despise your own prodigals or those in the world. Write them down and then engage by approaching those you have hurt or judged. Confess what you have said and done to hurt them and humbly ask forgiveness. We must deal with our own heart issues before we can help others with theirs. I sense God's anointing on the following:

When we begin to take our offenses toward our children seriously, they will begin to believe our good words and thoughts toward them now.

Dealing with a Sinning Brother. Matthew 18:15–20.

This is something we do not like to do. We fear someone might not like us or think we are judging them. My greatest failure as a pastor has been hesitating to lovingly confront people who live in error. We would rather not obey what Jesus said in verse 15 below. Many Christians, including pastors, act like they have cut this entire passage out of their Bibles. I have been guilty of this and have discovered that if we fail to nip sin in the bud, it becomes full grown, and we lose people through our neglect.

This is a passage we must study and show ourselves approved as workmen who do not need to be ashamed but who correctly handle the Word (This is my personal translation of 2 Timothy 2:15). We need to consider the entire text here, one portion at a time.

📖 "Moreover if your brother sins against you, **go and tell him** his fault between you and him alone. If he hears you, you have gained your brother. Matthew 18:15.

We get this backwards. We tell everyone *except* the one who offended us. The context concerns someone who has sinned against you personally. "Sins" comes from the Greek "Harmartese" which means "miss the mark of to err or sin against you."

A first line of defense is lovingly confronting a prodigal with how they have sinned against God and/or you personally. In the context of prodigals, Jesus tells us to approach them personally before we discuss them with someone else. (Other than the child's other parent.)

I could not find the word "faults" in Matthew 18:15 in my Greek Bible even though it is in the 1560 edition of the Geneva Bible and in twenty-five of the sixty-two other translations I considered in the free version of biblegateway.com. So, I turned to commentaries.

Matthew Henry Commentary gives further help. "Tell him his fault, *elenxon auton—argue the case with him*" (so the word signifies); "and do it with reason and argument, not with passion." Where the fault is plain and great, the person proper for us to deal with, and we have an opportunity for it, and there is no apparent danger of doing more hurt than good, we must with meekness and faithfulness tell people of what is amiss in them. Christian reproof is an ordinance of Christ for the bringing of sinners to repentance and must be managed as an ordinance. "Let the reproof be private, between thee and him alone; that it may appear you seek not his reproach, but his repentance." Note, it is a good rule, which should ordinarily be observed among Christians, not to speak of our brethren's faults to others, till we have first spoken of them to themselves, this would make less reproaching and more reproving; that is, less sin committed, and more duty done. It will be likely to work upon an offender, when he sees his reprover concerned not only for his salvation, in telling him his fault, but for his reputation in telling him of it privately. From Bible Gateway Matthew Henry's Commentary of Matthew 18:15–20.[1]

I sense Holy Spirit saying the right way to deal with someone who sins against you is to go to the person (if and when it is safe) and share the wrong you feel was done to you. The entire process brings things out in the open between the two of you to see if you can gain your prodigal brother or sister back. Hopefully, the two of you can have an open heartfelt discussion.

Verses sixteen and seventeen share two additional steps taken in hopes of bringing reconciliation.

📖 But if he will not hear, take with you one or two more, that 'by the mouth of two or three witnesses every word may be established.' [17] And if he refuses to hear them, tell *it* to the church. But if he refuses even to hear the church, let him be to you like a heathen and a tax collector. Matthew 18:16–17.

First, take one or two more people with you and try again to discuss the issues. If the prodigal still refuses to listen, tell the church. If the person will not listen to the church, whether as a whole or as represented by a council of elders or deacons, there is grounds to put the prodigal out of the church. We will discuss that in a following chapter.

Now, look at Matthew 18:18. Jesus assures us the battle is not over, even in the context of possible excommunication from a church for one who will not listen and repent.

📖 "Assuredly, I say to you, whatever you bind on earth will be bound in heaven, and whatever you loose on earth will be loosed in heaven. Mathew 18:18.

The Literal Translation Of The Bible Has: "Truly I say to you, Whatever you bind on the earth will be, **having been** bound in Heaven. And whatever you loose on the earth will be, **having been** loosed in Heaven." Matthew 18:18.

In other words, we find out the mind of God on a matter, i.e., concerning a prodigal who will not repent then we bind (forbid) what God forbids and Loose (permit) what God permits.

Verses 19–20 tell us to make this a matter of agreement with other Believers.

📖 "Again I say to you that if two of you agree on earth concerning anything that they ask, **it will be done** for them by My Father in heaven. ²⁰ For where two or three are gathered together in My name, I am there in the midst of them." Matthew 18:19–20.

What do you think would happen if small groups of parents of prodigals would gather in prayer each week and simply agree in prayer for each other's wayward children. No one understands such pain more than other parents of prodigals. You could pray before or after church or meet in homes now and then simply to see what God might do through Matthew 18:18–20 praying.

Let's move on to the final part of Matthew 18.

The Parable of the Unforgiving Servant. Vs. 21–35.

Redeeming prodigals is difficult, if not impossible, when parents and prodigals refuse to apply the work of forgiving grace with each other, which is why agreeing, binding, and loosing is so important. Let me share two germane passages before returning to Matthew 18.

> 📖 Pursue peace with all *people,* and holiness, without which no one will see the Lord: ¹⁵ looking carefully lest anyone fall short of the grace of God; **lest any root of bitterness** springing up cause trouble, and by this **many become defiled.** Hebrews 12:14–15.

The Bible tells us to guard our hearts with all diligence for out of it flow the issues of life (Proverbs 4:23). Few things are more trying on the heart than prodigals and/or parents who refuse to listen. We may believe we don't hold any offenses, but we don't see things in ourselves that others might.

In Matthew 18:21, Peter believed he exhibited exceptional grace. He had been taught we should forgive people when they sinned against us up to three times. He doubled the number, and then added one more when he questioned Jesus about how far he should go when it came to forgiving people who hurt him.

> 📖 Then Peter came to Him and said, "Lord, how often shall my brother sin against me, and I forgive him? Up to seven times?" Matthew 18:21.

Peter's "seven times" far exceeded what he had been taught. The Talmud says, "whoever seeks forgiveness from his friend should not seek it more than three times." Peter doubled that number and added one to it, "up to seven times?"

Jesus blew Peter's religious concept of forgiveness with his reply,

> 📖 Jesus said to him, "I do not say to you, up to seven times, but up to seventy times seven. Matthew 18:22.

Theologians do not believe Jesus was giving a limit of seventy times seventy times, which would be 490 times. He was saying we must learn to forgive other as God has forgiven us. Prodigals need to forgive their human and spiritual parents. Parents must forgive their children until reconciliation is possible. Jesus wanted His disciples to get this, so He gave the Parable of the unforgiving servant.

The first paragraph represents Abba Father's forgiving heart.

📖 Therefore the kingdom of heaven is like a certain king who wanted to settle accounts with his servants. 24 And when he had begun to settle accounts, one was brought to him who owed him ten thousand talents. 25 But as he was not able to pay, his master commanded that he be sold, with his wife and children and all that he had, and that payment be made. 26 The servant therefore fell down before him, saying, 'Master, have patience with me, and I will pay you all.' 27 Then the master of that servant was moved with compassion, released him, and forgave him the debt. Matthew 18:23–27.

When we are in Jesus, we are to become increasingly God-like. If we are becoming like Him, we will be ready to forgive our debtors as He forgives us. Consider the following verses.

📖 If we confess our sins, God is faithful and just to forgive our sins and cleanse us from all unrighteousness. 1 John 1:9.

📖 As far as the east is from the west, *So* far has He removed our transgressions from us. Psalm 103:12.

📖 "I, even I, am He who blots out your transgressions for My own sake; And I will not remember your sins. Isaiah 43:25.

The question here is whether or not our willingness to forgive others mirrors God's willingness to forgive us. Now, move on to the next verse in Matthew 18:28.

This verse represents human forgiveness apart from grace.

📖 "But that servant went out and found one of his fellow servants who owed him a hundred denarii; and he laid hands on him and took *him* by the throat, saying, 'Pay me what you owe!' Matthew 18:28.

It is easy to picture this man grabbing his fellow servant by the throat.

📖 So his fellow servant fell down at his feet and begged him, saying, 'Have patience with me, and I will pay you all.' 30 And he would not, but went and threw him into prison till he should pay the debt. Matthew 18:29–30.

How can one earn money in prison to pay a debt? This servant represents people who think they have the right to hang on to bitterness and punish their debtors until they repay their debts in full.

Isn't that how some parents and some prodigals behave? Heaven help us!

📖 So when his fellow servants saw what had been done, they were very grieved, and came and told their master all that had been done. 32 Then his master, after he had called him, said to him, 'You wicked servant! I forgave you all that debt because you begged me. 33 Should you not also have had compassion

on your fellow servant, just as I had pity on you?'
Matthew 18:31-33.

Deliverance ministers and counselors see a connection between bitterness, arthritis, and other diseases. Do you see it yet?

How many bitter people do you know who are happy and healthy?

📖 And his master was angry and delivered him to the torturers until he should pay all that was due to him. [35] "So My heavenly Father also will do to you if each of you, from his heart, does not forgive his brother his trespasses."
Matthew 18:34–35.

Jesus said His heavenly Father will turn each of us over to the torturers if we do not forgive those who sin against us. The torture may be mental, physical, financial, emotional, and/or relational.

One thing is sure—the torture will continue until your forgiveness is complete.

Right now, beginning with your own parents and/or children, I suggest you make mental notes of how they have hurt you and how they made you feel. If what they did or didn't do, still jerks you around emotionally, you are being tormented by things only you can deal with. Your only options are to either hold on to it and continue in torment or let go of it through forgiveness and be delivered from the torturer.

Make a bowl out of your hands and place in it the things your children or parents did to hurt you. Whisper those things in the bowl, along with the way those things made you feel. Take as long as it takes, even if you must continue this at home.

When you have finished placing things in the bowl, note how heavy it has become. You have a choice. You can refuse to forgive and carry the bowl until it kills you, or you can choose to forgive those who hurt you the most.

Forgiving does not mean putting yourself at risk for further abuse. It is forgiving others for the pain you already received from them.

When you are ready, choose to forgive the people for the pain they caused you and for how they made you feel. Renounce those feelings. They are liars and refuse to let you see how wonderful you really are. Once you have done this, picture Jesus standing nearby.

Jesus manifests His presence even more when two or three are gathered in His Name. He is ready to receive your bowls once your forgiveness is complete. Try to picture or imagine what Jesus does with your bowl when you give it to him.

Do the same thing with others (i.e., parents, pastors, children, friends, peers, bosses, fellow employees and whomever God brings to mind) who have hurt you. Most of all, take the lead in forgiving prodigals of every kind.

Prayer: Holy Spirit, I ask You to lead and guide me to make sure my forgiveness is complete, and I hold no anger or bitterness in my heart, beginning with my own parents and ancestors, as well as my children and any other prodigals in my life. In the Name of Jesus who freely offers total forgiveness to them and me, when we confess our sin and ask forgiveness. Amen.

Endnote:

[1] From Bible Gateway Matthew Henry's Commentary of Matthew 18:15–20.

Chapter Eleven: A Change of Natures

There is a difference between being born again and entering heaven with scarcely any reward and seeking first the Kingdom ~ which has the promise "All things will be added unto you."

We must own up to the reality many prodigals grew up in Christian homes, and received Jesus when they were young, etc. I am sure many of those who were saved as children will make it to heaven as through fire, but don't we want more for them and ourselves?

I've conducted way too many funerals for people who hoped their loved ones made it to heaven but were not sure. We certainly do not have access to the Book of Life to see whose names are written in it.

I think evangelism attempts fall short when all we do is have people pray a short little prayer after us and have them write the date they prayed in the front of their Bibles. Many people who minister in jails merely lead inmates in "The Prayer" that takes about 30 seconds to pray. No wonder we see them return to jail time after time. Doesn't such a life transforming decision deserve more effort than that?

I use the John 3:16 diagram which I first learned from Ralph Neighbour Jr. I stress the importance of making Jesus Lord and Master of one's life, using Romans 10:9–10 and 13.

I emphasize what Jesus said: if anyone wanted to come after Him they must take up their cross daily to truly follow Him. Once they understand this, I ask them, "What would it cost you to follow Jesus as Lord and Master?" A surprising number say "nothing." Some quote "by grace through faith" from Ephesians 2:8–9. In my opinion that is "cheap grace." The correct answer of what it costs to follow Jesus is "everything." When Jesus is Lord, our life consists of doing His will rather than our wants. The Bible teaches us to trust and obey. We are told to call on the Name of Jesus as Lord and Master.

The fun part comes when they understand making Jesus Lord means dying to self and doing what Jesus wants them to do. I always follow this with the question, "What has it cost you thus far NOT to follow and obey Jesus?" They usually mention incarceration, loss of freedom, loss of friends, income, family, etc. Our job of witnessing is not finished until people are following Jesus! Apart from that, some people may make it to heaven, yet as through fire.

📖 For no other foundation can anyone lay than that which is laid, which is Jesus Christ. [12] Now if anyone builds on this foundation *with* gold, silver, precious stones, wood, hay, straw, [13] each one's work will become clear; for the Day will declare it, because it will be revealed by fire; and the fire will test each one's work, of what sort it is. [14] If anyone's work which he has built on *it* endures, he will receive a reward. [15] If anyone's work is burned, he will suffer loss; **but he himself will be saved, yet so as through fire**. 1 Corinthians 3:11–15.

Kingdom life and victory comes from obeying King Jesus.

📖 But seek first the kingdom of God and His righteousness, and all these things shall be added to you. Matthew 6:33.

Which life do you hope for personally and for prodigals? We begin with a very sobering command from the Bible.

📖 Examine yourselves as to whether you are in the faith. Test yourselves. Do you not know yourselves, that Jesus Christ is in you?—unless indeed you are disqualified. 2 Corinthians 13:5.

The word "disqualified" refers to not standing the test of true salvation. I never want to cause anyone to doubt their faith. The only thing worse would be letting people slip into hell, unaware they have not become new creatures, when everything has been made new (2 Corinthians 5:17). Paul tells us to examine and test ourselves and make sure we are not disqualified. We also need to honestly examine prodigals to see if they are really in the faith. This chapter began with something God put on my heart to preach in a Reach the Forgotten jail service.

I began by asking the inmates: What nature have you? Do you have a divine, heavenly nature or a carnal, earthly nature? The answer reveals whether they are born from above or only from below. Is your nature good or bad? Happy or sad? Easy-going or mad? Carnal or spiritual? Carefree or worried? Naughty or nice? Are you a child of God or a child of the devil? Do you act more like Heavenly Father or your earthly father?

It depends on whether you have a spiritual nature or a soulish, earthly nature.

Are you spiritual or soulish? Are you a citizen of this world or a citizen of heaven? The Bible shares the story of one man's transformation from carnal to spiritual.

Peter started out carnal yet became spiritual. His faith moved him upward.

📖 Simon Peter, a servant and apostle of Jesus Christ, To those who through the righteousness of our God and Savior Jesus Christ have received **a faith as precious as ours**: [2] Grace and peace be yours in abundance through the knowledge of God and of Jesus our Lord. 2 Peter 1:1–2 NIV.

Peter writes so we might receive a faith as precious to you and me, as his was to him. You know, the faith that changed him from being up and down, faithful and unfaithful, walking on the water, only to sink kind of a guy. Saying he would never deny Jesus, then denying Him three times before the rooster crowed. Peter's life transitioned from carnal to spiritual after he repented, fully turned to God, and was filled with the Holy Spirit. His sermon on the Day of Pentecost reveals he had a new nature. His powerful, off-the-cuff sermon, in Acts 2:14–39 reveals he was no longer fearful of admitting he loved Jesus. He was finally able to talk the talk and walk the walk because of his new spiritual nature.

Jesus has a plan to restore glory to every life. A new nature is available!

📖 **His divine power** has given us **everything we need for a godly life** through our knowledge of him who called us by his own glory and goodness. 2 Peter 1:3 NIV.

We all begin life with an earthly nature because we are born in sin of parents who were born in sin. All have sinned and fallen short of the glory of God (Romans 3:23). We cannot walk a victorious spiritual life apart from God's DIVINE SANCTIFYING POWER.

God will give us a new spiritual nature if we take up our cross, deny ourselves daily, and follow Jesus. Refuse to give into soulishness where you rewrite the title of an old hymn to, "Take My Life and leave me be." Half-hearted commitment, victorious one day and back in sin the next, proves the need for God to do a work in a life only He can do.

Jesus said: If we seek to save our lives, we will lose them but if we give our lives to Him, and truly follow Him, He will save us. We will finally leave the sinful nature behind and walk with a new, spiritual, heavenly, conquering, and empowered nature.

Jesus calls us to participate in His divine nature!

📖 Through these he has given us his very great and precious promises, **so that through them YOU may participate in the divine nature, having escaped the corruption in the world caused by evil desires.** 2 Peter 1:4 NLV.

That is why Jesus could tell the man healed of paralysis in John 5:1–14 to go and SIN NO MORE! In John 8:1–11 He told the woman caught in the very act of adultery, to Go and SIN NO MORE! Anyone can escape the corruption of this world and participate in the divine nature, but it requires doing God's will, God's way, all the way.

Peter shared what he experienced personally. He discovered Jesus offers divine power to live Godly lives and participate in HIS heavenly nature. We, and every prodigal can escape the corruption of this world caused by evil desires: lust, addictions, revenge, pay backs, and so much more! I want to illustrate through three passages that compare a corrupt nature to a spiritual one.

The Corrupt, Carnal, Earthly Nature from 1 Corinthians 6:9–10

There are so many trapped in a corrupt nature; I call this the "O crap list." The Bible says if we do these things, they slam the door shut at the entrance to the Kingdom of God.

> 📖 Do you not know that the unrighteous will not inherit the kingdom of God? Do not be deceived. Neither fornicators, nor idolaters, nor adulterers, nor homosexuals, nor sodomites, [10] nor thieves, nor covetous, nor drunkards, nor revilers, nor extortioners will inherit the kingdom of God.
>
> 1 Corinthians 6: 9–10.

This verdict bans people from the Kingdom of God. It is imposed by the Court of Heaven. Once the judge strikes His gavel there is little hope of early release. Only God can make a way where there is no way. Thankfully, He did so, through Jesus!

**God's way is imputing a spiritual
heavenly nature through faith.**

📖 And such **were** some of you. But you were washed, but you were sanctified, but you were justified in the name of the Lord Jesus and by the Spirit of our God. 1 Corinthians 6: 11.

Some of us used to live in the "Cannot inherit the Kingdom" list. We WERE like that. We were stuck in a sin/confess, sin/confess earthly nature. But praise God—faith is our victory! When we believe and receive what Jesus did for us and begin walking in His divine nature, we can sing, "Victory in Jesus!" By faith we apply the power of Jesus' death sentence on the cross, and His subsequent rising from the dead to pay our fines in full and make it possible to participate in the divine nature. But we must believe and receive.

The Contrasting Sin Nature.

📖 But the cowardly, unbelieving, (sinners) abominable, murderers, sexually immoral, sorcerers, idolaters, and all liars shall have their part in the lake which burns with fire and brimstone, which is the second death." Revelation 21:8.

Pretty scary, don't you think? We need to view ourselves and prodigals as God does. It is both dangerous and hypocritical to apply verses like this to other people and their prodigals and not look at the mirror of coming face to face with God to see how we appear to Him.

📖 For now we see in a **mirror**, dimly, but then face to face. Now I know in part, but then I shall know just as I also am known. 1 Corinthians 13:12.

We need to seek a face to face with God encounter for us and our prodigals!

I realize this is a process. Nicodemus first came to Jesus by night. Peter made several decisions in following Jesus, and failed many times before becoming a mature, steadfast, and victorious leader.

Overcoming carnality by participating with Jesus' divine spiritual nature.

And He said to me, "It is done! I am the Alpha and the Omega, the Beginning and the End. I will give of the fountain of the water of life freely to him who thirsts. [7] He who overcomes shall inherit all things, and I will be his God and he shall be My son. Revelation 21:6–7.

Jesus spoke of two levels of living water:

The fountain of living water (salvation) is available to all through faith!

Jesus shared an encouraging truth with the Samaritan woman who had five husbands and was living with a man who was not her husband. She received it and became the town evangelist.

Jesus answered and said to her, "Whoever drinks of this water will thirst again, [14] but whoever drinks of the water that I shall give him will never thirst. But the water that I shall give him will become in him **a fountain of water** springing up into everlasting life." John 4:13–14.

Jesus says we shall inherit all things if we come to Him. Begin walking in His good and righteous spiritual nature, and overcome the old nature!

Rivers of living water (sanctifying baptism in Holy Spirit) is available to all by faith!

Jesus can and wants to sanctify us through and through. He is faithful and He will do it. Only He can do it!

📖 Now may the God of peace Himself sanctify you completely; and may your whole spirit, soul, and body be preserved blameless at the coming of our Lord Jesus Christ. [24] He who calls you *is* faithful, who also will do *it.*
1 Thessalonians 5:23–24.

I often ask Jesus to bring me into proper alignment so my body obeys my soul (mind, will, emotions, and identity). I submit my body to my soul and my soul to my human spirit and ask Jesus to fill me to overflowing with His Holy Spirit.

Jesus shed His blood on the cross and made a public spectacle of the principalities and powers that hold parents and prodigals in carnality. He triumphed over these devilish powers on the cross.

📖 Having wiped out the handwriting of requirements that was against us, which was contrary to us. And He has taken it out of the way, having nailed it to the cross. [15] Having disarmed principalities and powers, He made a public spectacle of them, triumphing over them in it. Colossians 2:14–16. (NKJV footnote states "handwriting" means "certificate of debt with us.")

We too can make a public spectacle of powers and principalities, but we must do it the same way Jesus did—by taking up our cross and going whole hog for His Kingdom.

The Works of the Earthly, Fleshly Sin Nature

Anyone caught in the lusts of the flesh must repent and turn to God if they want to take part in the Kingdom of God on earth and spend eternity in heaven. Nothing impure or unholy can enter the Kingdom. Baptism signifies dying with Christ, crucifying our sinful nature with Him.

You have to die to enter heaven, both now and later!

📖 Now the works of the flesh are evident, which are: adultery, fornication, uncleanness, lewdness, [20] idolatry, sorcery, hatred, contentions, jealousies, outbursts of wrath, selfish ambitions, dissensions, heresies, [21] envy, murders, drunkenness, revelries, and the like; of which I tell you beforehand, just as I also told *you* in time past, that those who practice such things **will not inherit the kingdom of God.** Galatians 5:19-21.

God said this, I didn't. And God never lies.

You are only kidding yourself if you think Galatians 5:19–21 speaks about others but not about you or your prodigal. It does not matter if you think you are saved, if you can quote Scriptures, speak in tongues, or prophesy. The Bible says you will not inherit the Kingdom of God if you practice the corrupt desires of your soulish nature. We are not supposed to judge one another, but the Bible flat out says we will not inherit the kingdom of God if we give way to our carnal, earthly natures. This is a matter of life and death, and not just physical death. It brings spiritual death and being thrown into hell where the fire does not go out and the worm does not die (Mark 9:48). You cannot take on a heavenly spiritual nature until the old nature is put to death. Paul taught this fact. God says you have to die to enter heaven.

📖 I have been crucified with Christ; it is no longer I who live, but Christ lives in me; and the *life* which I now live in the flesh

I live by faith in the Son of God, who loved me and gave Himself for me. Galatians 2:20.

Fruit-filled Spiritual Heavenly Nature

📖 But the fruit of the Spirit is love, joy, peace, longsuffering, kindness, goodness, faithfulness, [23]gentleness, self-control. Against such there is no law. [24]And those *who are* Christ's have crucified the flesh with its passions and desires. [25]If we live in the Spirit, let us also walk in the Spirit. Galatians 5:22–25.

Notice, I mentioned "Fruit-filled" not "fruity" spiritual nature. We wouldn't be studying prodigals and parents if there were not so many fruity behaviors to address. It is interesting to me this is the ninth major point in this chapter though I did not list them as points.

Galatians lists nine specific fruits produced through being connected to Jesus who describes Himself as the vine in John 15. If the fruit of the Spirit we just read about characterizes your life, or the life of your prodigal(s), it is evidence of a new nature, a spiritual nature. You and/or your prodigal have raised and are rising from death to life. Not so, if you manifest the old nature.

Some theologians believe love is the fruit of the Spirit and the other eight "fruits" flow from the single fruit of love. John 15:1–8 describes the importance of abiding in Jesus. When we do so, His fruit flows through our lives. When I tended a home orchard, I never saw a piece of fruit groaning or struggling to produce sweet fruit. Its sweetness came through being connected to the branch. This is a picture of being connected to Jesus.

Spiritual nature comes from an abiding connection to Jesus, the true vine.

Jesus said,

📖 "I am the true vine, and My Father is the vinedresser. ²Every branch in Me that does not bear fruit He takes away; and every *branch* that bears fruit He prunes, that it may bear more fruit. ³You are already clean because of the word which I have spoken to you. ⁴Abide in Me, and I in you. As the branch cannot bear fruit of itself, unless it abides in the vine, neither can you, unless you abide in Me. ⁵"I am the vine, you *are* the branches. He who abides in Me, and I in him, bears much fruit; for without Me you can do nothing. ⁶If anyone does not abide in Me, he is cast out as a branch and is withered; and they gather them and throw *them* into the fire, and they are burned. ⁷If you abide in Me, and My words abide in you, you will ask what you desire, and it shall be done for you. ⁸By this My Father is glorified, that you bear much fruit; so you will be My disciples. John 15:1–8.

Examine yourself and every prodigal. Is there evidence of being a new creation?

📖 Therefore, if anyone *is* in Christ, **he is** a new creation; old things *have passed* away; behold, all things **have become** new. 2 Corinthians 5:17.

Sinners can often quote verses like 2 Corinthians 5:17 and Acts 3:20 that tell us to repent and be converted so times of refreshing may come from the Lord. I say, "Show me your faith by your sincere works of repentance." Let me see your new spiritual nature!

It takes the terror of the Lord to convict some sinners.

📖 Therefore we make it our aim, whether present or absent, to be well pleasing to Him. [10] For we must all appear before the judgment seat of Christ, that each one may receive the things *done* in the body, according to what he has done, whether good or bad. [11] **Knowing, therefore, the terror of the Lord, we persuade men**; but we are well known to God, and I also trust are well known in your consciences.
2 Corinthians 5:9–11.

When I truly grasped the Gospel message and realized I was a sinner, it began the work of "scaring the hell" out of me. I remember reading about the moon turning red. The next morning, I walked to work in the dark, and the moon was blood red. My terror somewhat subsided when a true believer came to work, but I realized my need for a new spiritual nature to empower me to walk in holiness and freedom from sin and fear of death.

It is a mistake to protect prodigals from immediate harm, only to lose them to complete destruction. It is a mistake to protect children from the discipline of their parents, teachers, or the law. Those who do the crime should spend the time. Those who are not trained by righteous discipline are likely to continue in sin until they die and face eternity without Christ. We must do everything possible to make sure prodigals are truly converted.

Many Decisions — One True Conversion

A large evangelistic association sadly admitted a low percentage of those who came forward at crusades showed significant life change. They never began attending church or living renewed lives after they made a decision to come to the altar. People often make many small decisions and take many small steps toward Christ before they experience authentic, life changing, conversion.

When we meet Nicodemus in John Chapter Three, he already had made the decision that he wanted to know more about Jesus. Though he was very religious, he needed true conversion. He needed Jesus to break free from an earthly nature to a heavenly one.

📖 There was a man of the Pharisees named Nicodemus, a ruler of the Jews. John 3:1.

The Pharisees were a spiritual order who believed in angels and demons and life after death. Nicodemus was also a member of the Sanhedrin. He was like policeman and detective rolled up in one. He knew the Old Testament law and had the power to enforce it against Jewish people who failed to follow their Law. Some sources say Nicodemus was very young and the richest Pharisee. Theologians believe Nicodemus who came to Jesus by night was the rich young ruler who had to choose between riches and eternal life.

Secretive Seeking

Prodigals may be seeking truth but do not want anyone to know it. Perhaps that is why so many are seeking "truth" in wrong places. Thankfully, Nicodemus looked to Jesus.

📖 This man came to Jesus by night and said to Him, "Rabbi, we know that You are a teacher come from God; for no one can do these signs that You do unless God is with him." John 3:2.

Nicodemus was impressed with Jesus' teachings and signs and wonders. (Signs point you to The Son!) Nicodemus knew God was working through Jesus. But He waited to approach after dark so no one would associate him with this radical teacher. Jesus cut through the chase.

📖 Jesus answered and said to him, "Most assuredly, I say to you, unless one is born again, he cannot see the kingdom of God." John 3:3.

Nicodemus thought, "you've got to be kidding." "Impossible, No way!" Jesus knew Nicodemus, better than Nicodemus knew himself. Nic was a highly respected leader. He was respectable and followed the law. But he was born of earthly, soulish, selfish nature, just like his parents. His religion wasn't enough to enter the Kingdom of God.

📖 Nicodemus said to Him, "How can a man be born when he is old? Can he enter a second time into his mother's womb and be born?" John 3:4.

All Nicodemus understood was physical birth.
He had no clue of spiritual birth.

He like everyone else, was born with an earthly, sinful nature, incapable of pleasing God or walking in victory. Nicodemus was born physically. But the only cure for his condition was being born again spiritually so he could partake of the divine nature.

📖 Jesus answered, "Most assuredly, I say to you, unless one is born of water and the Spirit, he cannot enter the kingdom of God. ⁶ That which is born of the flesh is flesh, and that which is born of the Spirit is spirit. John 3:5–6.

Some people wrongly think being born of water refers to baptism. It does not refer to water baptism, though baptism is an act of faith and obedience for people after salvation.

**Being born of water means being born physically.
It brings physical birth.**

When a woman's bag of water breaks, it is time to stop whatever you are doing and head to the hospital. You don't stop at McDonalds for a quarter pounder or at Starbucks for coffee. You rush to the hospital because you know a baby is about to be born physically, with the same natural, sinful, fleshly nature his parents were born with. "There is none righteous, no not one" (Psalm 53:1–3, Romans 3:10–12).

Jesus told this important religious ruler,

**"You must be born spiritually too, not just physically,
in order to participate in the divine nature."**

Until a person is born again, he/she is caught in the corrupt nature. The same is true of prodigals. That which is born of the Spirit is spirit. The Good News is: "Your spirit can be born again, and you can live a spiritual life!" You may have done some good works, but you cannot have a divine nature until your spirit is born again and God's Holy Spirit takes up residence in your life.

Examine the evidence for yourself and for your prodigal! Do your lives, temperament, victory over sin and temptation testify to a spiritual nature or a corrupt nature?

I do not have time to unpack the 1 John 3:4–9, other than saying it is written in the present ongoing sense and is not referring to a slip up here and there.

📖 Whoever commits sin also commits lawlessness, and sin is lawlessness. ⁵ And you know that He was manifested to take away our sins, and in Him there is no sin. ⁶ **Whoever abides in Him does not sin**. Whoever sins has neither seen Him nor known Him. 1 John 3:4–6.

📖 ⁷ Little children, let no one deceive you. He who practices righteousness is righteous, just as He is righteous. ⁸ *He who sins is of the devil,* for the devil has sinned from the beginning. For this purpose the Son of God was manifested, that He might destroy the works of the devil. ⁹ Whoever has been born of God does not sin, for His seed remains in him; and he cannot sin, because he has been born of God.
1 John 3:7–9.

Evangelists sometimes say, "You can't get a person saved until they know they are lost." The weight of the Canon of Scripture says if we continue in sin, we simply are not right with God. If we participate in the corrupt nature, we need help moving into His Divine Nature. Think of what Jesus said to Nicodemus.

📖 Do not marvel that I said to you, 'You must be born again.' ⁸ The wind blows where it wishes, and you hear the sound of it, but cannot tell where it comes from and where it goes. So is everyone who is born of the Spirit." John 3:7–8.

Holy Spirit shouts this warning to each of us and every prodigal.

📖 Beware, brethren, lest there be in any of you an evil heart of unbelief in departing from the living God; ¹³ but exhort one another daily, while it is called "Today," lest any of you be hardened through the deceitfulness of sin. ¹⁴ For we have become partakers of Christ if we hold the beginning of our confidence steadfast to the end. Hebrews 3:12–13.

If you sense the wind of the Spirit is blowing in your direction— confess your sinful, soulish, carnal nature. Cry out to the Lord and repent of your sins. Believe in Jesus and what He did for you. Receive Him and His Spirit so you can step into a new life.

Call on the Name of the Lord and you will become a new creature. The old will be gone and you will be born again and walk in newness of life. Do this and . . .

YOU can participate in the divine nature, having escaped the corruption in the world caused by evil desires.

Prayer Points for Prodigals from this chapter:
- ➢ Pray they will hunger and thirst for Kingdom life.
- ➢ Pray they will want to participate in the Divine Nature.
- ➢ Pray they will have faith to move them upward.
- ➢ Pray they will desire to take up their cross and follow Jesus as Lord.
- ➢ Pray God will restore His glory to their lives.
- ➢ Pray God will open their eyes to witness carnal nature and consequences.
- ➢ Pray they will contrast selfish sinful nature to true spiritual nature.
- ➢ Pray they will overcome carnality with Jesus' divine nature.
- ➢ Pray for their true salvation (Fountain of Living Water).
- ➢ Pray for rivers of living water (Holy Spirit baptism and sanctification).

➢ Pray they will abide in Jesus and His fruit will flow through them.

➢ Pray they learn to abide in Jesus.

➢ Pray they will examine themselves to see if they are new creatures.

➢ Pray the terror of the Lord will make the error of their ways evident.

➢ Pray for true spiritual birth unto a new spiritual nature.

➢ Pray they grasp the consequence of ongoing sin.

➢ Pray they grasp the reward of Kingdom life.

Take a moment to ask Holy Spirit: "What are you saying to me through this chapter?" Jot down any thoughts He gives you and pray; make them a matter of prayer and meditation.

Prayer: Father, protect the reader from false condemnation or fear of not being born again. At the same time, we ask You to show us every place further cleansing is needed. Thank you for being faithful and just to forgive us of our sins and cleanse us fully.

Chapter Twelve: Going to War for Prodigals

This chapter and the next transitions into a call to engage in the battle for prodigals.

**"What are we willing to do to rescue prodigals?
Will we pay the price to bring them home to Jesus?**

Let's begin with some good news. Jesus wants us to take a stand between prodigals and Satan. As intercessors we stand between heaven and prodigals to draw them closer to each other. God blesses such prayer greatly.

There is also some bad news. Satan resists us when we stand in the gap for prodigals. We must stand in the gap between Satan and prodigals, praying against their agreement with the devil and Satan's hold on them. This requires dedicated prayer and intercession.

Four days prior to writing this I had a man come for deliverance. The devil had a legal right to torment him because he had been involved with pornography. He was horribly traumatized. I led him in confession and renouncing sin, and breaking soul ties. Then I began something that really ticked the devil and his demons off. I commenced commanding the demons of lust and pornia to come out. They screamed through an angry rebellious man's voice, "No, he belongs to me, I own him." Such hatred was spewing through the man's face, eyes, and voice, it took me back for a second. It was an unscheduled appointment, and I was attacked with a lie I could not do much because I didn't have an intercessor to help pray. I didn't like being where I was at that moment, but I pressed in, took authority, and the demons did come out.

**I've learned, we must not grow weary in well-doing
or fall back when we come against the enemy.**

Praying for prodigals, especially those who are demonized, is not a pleasant pastime, but we may be the only one who knows and loves them well enough to take a risk for them.

So, will we take up our crosses daily and follow Jesus as He calls us to? (Matthew 16:24–25; Mark 8:34, 10:21, and Luke 9:23–24.). I decree: "when we truly take up our crosses and follow Jesus all the way, we will see prodigals returning home en masse." I sense God will use parents of prodigals to reach the prodigals of other parents.

As we learn to better stand in the gap for our prodigals and the prodigals of this world, we will witness God's will being done God's way. The weapons of our warfare are not carnal, but mighty. We must doers, not just hearers, of God's will and going God's way!

We need to stand in the gap to break delusion off Prodigals.

Prodigals often live in a dream world. They think they will make it to heaven even though they commit sins the Bible says will land them in hell. They think they will find the dream job, have plenty of money, and can continue walking away from God and from those who care for them, without consequence. They may think there are many roads to heaven. They live in delusion until we break it off them. Listen to what the wisest man ever wrote.

📖 Do you see a man wise in his own eyes? *There is* more hope for a fool than for him. Proverbs 26:12.

One warning is so important, God repeats it in Proverbs.

📖 There is a way *that seems* right to a man, But its end *is* the way of death. Proverbs 16:25.

Without intervention, prodigals fail to recognize or admit the folly of their ways.

They will blame their problems on their parents, pastors, schools, etc. We must pray prophetically as we intercede for prodigals. We dare not just accept things as they are. We must pray God's prophetic purpose into prodigals. Ezekiel scolds Israel for not standing in the gap. A gap represents a breach in the wall.

📖 O Israel, your prophets are like foxes in the deserts. [5] **You have not gone up into the gaps to build a wall** for the house of Israel to stand in battle on the day of the Lord. [6] They have envisioned futility and false divination, saying, 'Thus says the Lord!' But the Lord has not sent them; yet they hope that the word may be confirmed. Ezekiel 13:4–6.

Foxes are similar to house cats. They will fix their focus on something and be unaware of the danger around them. Ezekiel compares prophets to foxes who are not aware of the need to stand in the gap to prevent danger.

There was a wonderful man, named Vere, in my second church who had gifts of serving and helps. He was a farmer, complete with a henhouse. He made a contraption where people could drive up to a conveyer near his henhouse. They could deposit their coins for a dozen eggs, and they would receive their eggs at their car window. People loved the convenience and did not cheat his system.

There was a thief, however, in the form of a fox that would raid his henhouse. One day he was plowing a field and noticed a fox totally engrossed in something it was trying to catch in a fence row. He stopped the tractor, put it in neutral and set the brakes, but left it running. He then pulled a bar out of his toolbox, snuck up behind the fox and dispatched that thief once for all.

We must intentionally see the dangers assaulting prodigals and stand in the gap for them. It is urgent we hear God's voice concerning prodigals so we can stand in the gap on their behalf. God is not willing that any should perish (2 Peter 3:9). He wants every prodigal to come to repentance, but both parents and prodigals are free to do good or evil. Everyone will always reap what they sow, and more than they sow, for good or bad. (Galatians 6:7–8)

There are three strong determiners for every life. God, who truly wants to bless. Satan who wants to steal, kill, and destroy. The third determiner is each individual because he or she has the final say in their personal life. Still, Believers can change the way things are through dedicated prayer, intercession, and spiritual warfare. We can speak into and pray on behalf of prodigals.

God never forgets the human component.

We must never forget the God component.

God's heart for prodigals is seen in the Parables of the Lost Sheep, Lost Coin, and prodigal son. God's heart is for every prodigal to be redeemed and come home. But God will not force His will on them. Parents and prodigals cannot do it without God and He will not do it without them. God gave dominion and authority over the earth realm to humans. Satan stole that from Adam and Eve. But, praise God, Jesus bought our authority and dominion back when He triumphed over Satan on the cross. Therefore, Jesus said, "All authority on heaven and earth have been given to me; therefore, YOU GO and make disciples of all nations and people groups. That includes prodigals!

Do you think our omnipotent God always gets what He wants? Not so, because God does not forget the free will and human responsibility and consequences.

One of the most interesting passages in the Bible shares when God did not get His desired result for His prodigal nation.

God speaks clearly to the condition of prodigals.

📖 The people of the land have used oppressions, committed robbery, and mistreated the poor and needy; and they wrongfully oppress the stranger. Ezekiel 22:29.

Does that not describe the condition of many prodigals? Some homeless prodigals sneak into apartment buildings and sleep in their hallways. Others may take whatever they can get with little thought or concern for God or their own children. God gives a call to the only ones who can make a difference for prodigals—those who care for prodigals.

📖 So I sought for a man among them who would make a wall, and **stand in the gap** before Me on behalf of the land, **that I should not destroy it; but I found no one.** Ezekiel 22:30.

The word "man" here certainly is not limited to males. The Sovereign omniscient God knew exactly what was needed. It would take someone, anyone, who would stand in the gap so He would not have to destroy a prodigal nation!

It required human intercession.

Think of how Moses interceded for his nation and for his brother and sister when they strayed from the Lord. Unfortunately, in Ezekiel's day, no one stepped up to the call to stand in the gap. Therefore, God had no choice but to release His wrath. He did not get what He wanted. This applies to prodigal children and prodigal nations who never turn back to God.

📖 Therefore I have poured out My indignation on them; I have consumed them with the fire of My wrath; and I have recompensed their deeds on their own heads," says the Lord God. Ezekiel 22:31.

Before we proceed, I ask you to join me in a decree we learned from Derek Prince. My wife and I make this decree each morning and evening and enjoy The Lord's protection throughout our days and nights.

I am redeemed by the blood of the Lamb
from the hand of the enemy!

Now, let me share biblical strategy for standing in the gap on behalf of prodigal children, states, and nations. I want to unpack some overlooked Scriptures which are designed by God to instruct us how to stand in the gap on behalf on individual prodigals and prodigal states and nations. This strategy takes commitment and consistency, but it works!

Tearing down veils the god of this age uses to hold captives captive.

📖 But even if our gospel is veiled, it is veiled to those who are perishing, ⁴ whose minds the god of this age has blinded, who do not believe, lest the light of the gospel of the glory of Christ, who is the image of God, should shine on them. 2 Corinthians 4:3–4.

Let me break this down phrase by phrase.

The god of this age has veiled the eyes of prodigals.

Satan has veiled their eyes to the Gospel—the Good News of complete redemption. God wants to save every prodigal from the gutter most to the uttermost. The god of this age has blinded their eyes to prevent this.

This veil keeps lost people from seeing and being saved.

Veil comes from the Greek word "kalupto." This veil is a literal veil, much like the skin that covers our bodies. Satan uses the veil so prodigals cannot see. It is not that they do not want to see or will not see. They cannot see. Consider the following translation.

📖 The god of this age has **blinded the minds** of unbelievers, so that they **cannot see** the **light** of the gospel that displays the glory of Christ, who is the image of God. 2 Corinthians 4:4 NIV.

The god of this age has blinded their minds.

Let me expound on this. "The god of this age has blinded their minds so they cannot think straight." Isn't that true of prodigals?

It is also worth noting here, the Greek language uses the prefix "a" like English uses "un." English reverses the meaning of words with "un" like unfaithful, unfruitful, unproductive, etc. The Greek uses "a" before "kulupto" to reverse its meaning. The Greek word for revelation is "ap-po-al-oop-sis" which adds the negative to "kulupto" so it literally means "unveiling." We can stand in the gap for prodigals and remove the veils from their minds and eyes so they can receive divine revelation!

We can open the aperture of a prodigal's soul so they can see.

The Greek word translated "light" in 2 Corinthians 4:4 is "photismos" which is the root word for photography. When we take a photo, we point the lens toward our subject, hit the button and the aperture opens so the light comes in to make an imprint. As we stand in the gap and pray for our prodigal's blinded mind and eyes to be open, the aperture of their soul is snapped open, and the good news of Jesus can then be imprinted there, on their souls!

We can pray they receive a baptism in love.

📖 For the love of Christ compels us, because we judge thus: that if One died for all, then all died; [15] and He died for all, that those who live should live no longer for themselves, but for Him who died for them and rose again.
2 Corinthians 5:14–15.

Prodigals often do not feel loved by God, their parents, spouses, or others—even when they are deeply loved. They don't even love themselves. They believe a lie like the devil told Eve, beginning with the question "Did God really say. . ..? Prodigals may believe God loves others . . . just not them. So, they often fall into one bad relationship after another looking for love only God can give. They lose themselves in relationships that promise free love but lead to bondage and heartache.

As we pray against the hardness of their hearts, we can also pray for God's love to soften their hearts. We can break bondages off their emotions and command spirits of emotional coldness to let them go and leave, in Jesus' Name.

We can decree Scriptures over prodigals.

The concept of decreeing desired ends over people is more common in some circles than others. Some translations use the word "declare" and others use "decree," but the promise of both decree and declare is to speak something until it is established.

📖 You will make your prayer to Him, He will hear you, And you will pay your vows. [28] **You will also declare a thing, And it will be established for you**; So light will shine on your ways. [29] When they cast *you* down, and you say, 'Exaltation *will come!'* Then He will save the humble *person.* Job 22:28–29.

Jesus said we could speak in faith to a mountain or fig tree, "be moved" and it will move (Matthew 17:20, Luke 17:6).

Decreeing is powerful in both negative and positive ways.

Like many people, Job brought evil upon himself by speaking his fears. He feared something would happen to his children, his wealth, and his health, and what he spoke became his reality (Job

3:25). We mistakenly do this with prodigals. We decree things like, "You're going to end up in jail," and they end up there.

I have ministered in a county jail at least once a month for over three decades. I often question inmates, "When you were young, did people tell you, 'You are going to end up in jail?'" A huge majority always answer "yes." Such is the power of decree. Noting the power of decree, I will conclude this chapter with a few Scriptures and decrees you can make over yourself and prodigals. You may want to earmark this section and continue decreeing each one until they finish their good work.

What you decree will be established!

📖 Therefore, from now on, we regard no one according to the flesh. Even though we have known Christ according to the flesh, yet now we know *Him thus* no longer.
2 Corinthians 5:16.

➢ I decree I will no longer view prodigals according to their carnal nature. I will decree God's divine prophetic nature over them.

📖 Therefore, if anyone *is* in Christ, *he is* a new creation; old things have passed away; behold, all things have become new. 2 Corinthians 5:17.

➢ I decree (insert name) will become a new creation in Christ. The old will pass away, all things will become new.

📖 Now all things *are* of God, who has reconciled us to Himself through Jesus Christ, and has given us the ministry of reconciliation, ¹⁹ that is, that God was in Christ reconciling the

world to Himself, not imputing their trespasses to them, and has committed to us the word of reconciliation.
2 Corinthians 5:18–19.

➢ I decree I will walk in my ministry of reconciliation for prodigals. I will not impute their sins unto them but will speak decrees of reconciliation over them.

📖 For though we walk in the flesh, we do not war according to the flesh. 2 Corinthians 10:3.

➢ I decree I will not battle for prodigals according to my earthly and carnal nature. I will war from my sanctified spiritual nature.

📖 For the weapons of our warfare *are* not carnal (of the flesh) but mighty in God for pulling down strongholds.
2 Corinthians 10:4.

➢ I declare I will no longer walk according to my hurt, worried, anxious, or fearful flesh. Instead, I decree I will pray and decree according to the Word of God and the God of the Word.

I found a quote about strongholds from my Building Blocks of Deliverance Seminar. I believe it is something Barbara Yoder said in a conference we attended years ago at Shekinah Church in Ann Arbor, Michigan.

A stronghold is a mindset impregnated with hopelessness about something that denies the Word of God and results in faithlessness, and a place of darkness that we have no hope for.

Take a moment and let God bring to your attention any mindsets you or prodigals have that are pregnant with hopelessness. Jot down mindsets preventing you personally from decreeing the positive things you desire for your prodigal.

Before making a decree, confession may be in order.

➤ I decree the weapons of my warfare are mighty in God for pulling down strongholds, wrong mindsets, darkness, and faithlessness.

➤ Lord, I confess nagging and fretting has compounded problems rather than solving them. This day I declare I will use strong and mighty weapons in God to pull down the strongholds holding prodigals in bondage to sin, Satan, and self.

📖 Casting down arguments and every high thing that exalts itself against the knowledge of God, bringing every thought into captivity to the obedience of Christ. 2 Corinthians 10:5.

The Greek word translated "casting down" means "take down, pull down, depose, and destroy." The Greek word, translated "arguments" is the word "logismous." The English word "logic" comes from this. It is Strongs Greek # 3053 and is defined as: "Reasoning, thinking; a conception, device. From logizomai; computation, i.e., reasoning."

Verse 5 refers to using prayer and declaration to demolish the devil's logic systems working against prodigals.

The devil wants us to complain about the faulty logic systems prodigals have. God wants us to demolish them through decrees and declaration.

➢ In Jesus' Mighty Name, I decree I am now tearing down every faulty reasoning of _____ (name the prodigal you are praying for) and taking their thoughts captive to the obedience of Christ and his plan for his/her life. (You may want to target specific logic systems. For example, target things like, "I'm my own boss," "Nobody can tell me what to do." "Being right in their own eyes." Promises of comfort through drugs, alcohol, drugs, etc."

**Such intercession and warfare begin
with those closest to a prodigal.**

Parents and spouses are **not** given the warning "Do not try this at home!" Many problems begin in the home and can be first addressed in the home. I wrote the book *Breaking Patterns of Perversity ~ Freedom from Iniquity*[1] to help individuals, parents, and professional counselors address particular bents and distortions of character, they or their children or counselees have. Less than a week previous this writing, a well-respected family counselor called and testified how useful that book is in helping her clients break long-standing patterns of negative behavior. Isn't that what we want for our prodigals?

So, do all you can do, and if that isn't enough, seek further assistance. We must not give up until prodigals have returned to God and their families. The first jail chaplain I served under often said, "Don't give up on him! Aren't you glad Jesus never gave up on you?"

**Once those who are closest to prodigals obey God's plan of
standing in the gap for them, they have done their part.**

When that doesn't work call upon the Ekklesia, if the prodigal still refuses to repent.

📖 And being ready to punish all disobedience when your obedience is fulfilled. 2 Corinthians 10:6.

Paul said he was ready to punish all disobedience of prodigals when the Church of Corinth did everything, he asked the local Ekklesia, (governmental body referred to as "church") to do.

The phrase "to Punish" in 2 Corinthians 10:6 literally means to give justice over, defend, avenge, vindicate, retaliate, or punish every act of disobedience. Interestingly, the Greek word translated disobedience can mean, disobedience, imperfect hearing, or inattention.

Punishment usually gravitates from the least restrictive to increasingly restrictive punishment. For example, if you get stopped for speeding, you may get off with just a warning. If you get stopped for speeding a second time, you will probably get a ticket and a minor fine. If you continue getting pulled over for speeding the punishment will undoubtedly increase. Fines for repeated offenses will become higher and jail time may be likely.

God will call leaders to step in and God will inflict harsher action so prodigals will come to their senses and repent.

That will be the topic of the next chapter.

Endnote:
[1] Dr. Douglas E Carr, *Breaking Patterns of Perversity ~ Freedom from Iniquity.* KDP 2022.

Chapter Thirteen:
Drastic Measures for Parents & Prodigals

Since this final chapter is so serious, I share a story, hoping you will begin with a laugh.

I'll Get It

Three Elderly ladies were discussing the trials of getting older.

One said, "Sometimes I catch myself holding a jar of mayonnaise in front of the refrigerator, and I can't remember whether I need to put it away or start making a sandwich.

The second lady chimed in, "Sometimes I find myself on the landing of the stairs and I can't remember if I was on my way up or on my way down."

The third lady said, "I don't have those problems; knock on wood." She raps her knuckles on the table, pauses, then gets up. "That must be the door."[1]

My sincere hope and desire is this chapter is not necessary. I feel like a parent whose adult child is in trouble with the law and facing a prison sentence. After thirty-five years of ministry in the

Branch County Jail, my heart for the broken, disenfranchised, and those who are sick or in prison should be obvious. I care for their parents too. We must learn to do God's will, God's way. God's will is always right but not always easy.

I have pondered quitting jail ministry several times. I have a busy schedule and it takes time and money to drive to another city nearly every week to either preach to inmates, or counsel them one on one. Every time I have considered quitting, however, I've sensed Jesus saying, "In as much as you have done it to the least of these my brethren, you have done it unto me." I simply can't quit on Jesus, and Jesus will not quit on prodigals!

That does not mean Jesus will not discipline them—severely if need be. The first chaplain I served under often asked how certain former inmates were doing. Sometimes I had to give a negative report, and he would say, "Don't give up! Aren't you glad Jesus never gave up on you?" May God grant us such perseverance for prodigals.

We must learn to do God's will, God's way.

David C. McCasland wrote the single session Bible Study "The Severe Mercy of God." He discussed, "What happens to a person who truly receives the mercy of God?" I quote his opening paragraph.

> Mercy has been defined as "kindness in excess of what may be expected by fairness." If God had been only fair and just with each of us, where would we be? But is there a harshness in God's mercy—like a doctor's frank diagnosis that precedes healing? Are there "conditions" for receiving God's mercy? Why do so many people refuse it?

What happens to a person who truly receives the mercy of God? [2]

Trying to refresh a quote I partly remembered, I searched the web.

Here is what I found: "Desperate times call for desperate measures. Quote by Obert Skye." He wrote,

"Desperate times call for desperate measures." That's a saying, or a bit of advice, or a catchphrase, or a string of words used to confuse people less intelligent than you. In any case, it means: Life is tough, so you'd better fight hard- or something like that"— Obert Skye, *Leven Thumps and the Whispered Secret.*[3]

There are times when life is tough in homes, families, and churches. There are times when doing the right thing feels wrong, and in our attempts to reach prodigals and bring them home, we may think the easy thing is best. God does not call us to do the easy thing. He calls us to do whatever it takes to reach prodigals. Solomon offers great advice.

📖 Trust in the Lord with all your heart, And lean not on your own understanding; [6] In all your ways acknowledge Him, And He shall direct your paths. Proverbs 3:5–6.

This passage lays 75% of the responsibility on us. WE need to trust with all our hearts, WE need to acknowledge Him in all our ways, and WE need to lean not on our own understanding. If and when we do our 75%, God will make our paths straight. So, do we truly want God to direct our paths concerning prodigals? His ways are higher than our ways, are they not? God loves every prodigal even more than we do. His eternal parental nature is so good, loving, kind, and merciful, He gave His only begotten Son that we and our prodigals might not perish but have everlasting life!

The Message translates this passage in its larger context as follows,

📖 Trust God from the bottom of your heart; don't try to figure out everything on your own. Listen for God's voice in everything you do, everywhere you go; he's the one who will keep you on track. Don't assume that you know it all. Run to God! Run from evil! Your body will glow with health, your very bones will vibrate with life! Honor God with everything you own; give him the first and the best. Your barns will burst, your wine vats will brim over. But don't, dear friend, resent God's discipline; don't sulk under his loving correction. It's the child he loves that God corrects; a father's delight is behind all this. Proverbs 3:5–12 MSG.

I mused on this chapter for a couple of weeks before I was ready to share the words God placed on my heart. This is a difficult subject to discuss.

Therefore, let me share a couple of things God spoke to me before we launch into the meat of this chapter. First, in the New Testament it was the church, not parents, who had the responsibility to hand unrepentant prodigals over to Satan so they might learn not to blaspheme. But then God reminded me of a very serious Old Testament Passage.

📖 "If a man has a stubborn and rebellious son who will not obey the voice of his father or the voice of his mother, and who, when they have chastened him, will not heed them, [19] then his father and his mother shall take hold of him and bring him out to the elders of his city, to the gate of his city. [20] And they shall say to the elders of his city, 'This son of ours is stubborn and rebellious; he will not obey our voice; he is a glutton and a drunkard.' [21] Then all the men of his city shall stone him to death with stones; so you shall put away the evil from among you, and all Israel shall hear and fear. Deuteronomy 21:18–21.

Perhaps you can imagine how much stress a parent had already experienced before coming to the point of conviction where he/she was ready to turn a rebellious child over to the elders of the city. It must have been incredibly difficult even after suffering years of disrespect, rebellion, and wanton living from the child.

I balance this extreme passage with something God spoke to me while I was driving into the office early in the morning before working on this chapter. I was thinking of some men I had poured a lot into. They refuse to follow my counsel, feign sincere repentance, but continue in drunkenness, misusing drugs, and promiscuous behavior. They seem to think they can call or drop in whenever they wish. They keep on calling, asking for prayer, counsel, help of all sorts, but seldom invest a minute or dollar in helping their parents or building our ministry.

After receiving multiple calls on my day off, even though I have politely asked that they not bother me unless it is an emergency, I was close to reacting rather than responding to their demands. I admit I was a tad miffed because they don't seem to know or care how heavy my load is. They expect me to do things for them even though they are not faithful to the church we pastor and contribute little or nothing. I was having one of those "I've had it moments" and imagined myself saying to one of them, "I don't owe you anything."

God immediately intercepted my pity party.

He said, "Owe no man anything but love!" (Romans 13:8). He then reviewed my personal history from the late eighties when I backslid. He shot questions at me as from a machine gun, "Did I love you when you were running from me and living in sin? Did I love you when I disciplined you with accidents, tickets, sky-high insurance? Did I love you through your severe closed head injury from being dragged by a horse? Did I love you through cluster headaches and financial ruin? Did I love you to spiritual, emotional, relational, and physical health?"

I lowered my head and thanked the Lord for His chastising. Yes, He loved me even when I ignored Him! God loved me when I was at my worst. As God loves us, we are to love others. We need to love them enough to discipline them. So, after a long introduction, let's brace ourselves for the Word of God.

Paul instructed the Corinthians to kick a man out of Church.

Some churches lower their standards to attract large crowds. Paul wasn't into building big crowds. He wanted to build big people! He poured into strong disciples who planted strong churches to build strong Christians. They even did so when they were so small in number, they met in homes. Paul did not instruct the church with a "better than thou attitude." He did, however, call Christians and churches to be holy, perfect, and without blemish, ready for the Lord's return. Consider Paul's heart and goal in 1 Corinthians 2:1–5:

📖 And I, brethren, when I came to you, did not come with excellence of speech or of wisdom declaring to you the testimony of God. (Footnote, "mystery" of God.) 2 For I determined not to know anything among you except Jesus Christ and Him crucified. ³ I was with you in weakness, in fear, and in much trembling. ⁴ And my speech and my preaching *were* not with persuasive words of human wisdom, **but in demonstration of the Spirit and of power,** ⁵ **that your faith should not be in the wisdom of men but in the power of God.**
1 Corinthians 2:1–5.

Endless words and finding fault does not help prodigals. You can talk to them until you are blue in the face (totally exasperated), but that is not enough. Weeks and months of doing so has proven that futile. They need powerful evidence from God Almighty. They need to see the power of God at work in good ways, including painful ways at times. Paul calls us to faith through the power of God, not the so-called wisdom of man. He was willing to take a stand for everyone's good.

I remind you it was the Prodigal Son's Father who loved his son so much; he let him experience the consequences of his ways. Once the prodigal's father stepped out of the way, God used the son's suffering to bring him to full repentance. Paul wanted every Believer to have faith in the power of God, not the so-called wisdom of man. He was willing to take a stand for everyone's good. I remind you it was the Prodigal Son's Father who loved his son so much; he let him experience the consequences of his ways. Once the prodigal's father stepped out of the way, God used the son's suffering to bring him to full repentance.

Handing him over to Satan let him face the consequences.

We will first examine two passages in where Apostle Paul speaks of handing prodigals over to Satan. I will point out heaven's purpose in such severe mercy.

📖 In the name of our Lord Jesus Christ, when you are gathered together, along with my spirit, with the power of our Lord Jesus Christ, [5] deliver such a one to Satan for the destruction of the flesh, that his spirit may be saved in the day of the Lord Jesus. [6] Your glorying *is* not good. Do you not know that a little leaven leavens the whole lump?
1 Corinthians 5:4–6.

This is one of those places where Believers tend to ignore what Scripture says, or take it to extremes. It is important we understand what the Word of God tells us to do, and why.

Paul takes delivering a prodigal over to Satan seriously.

I can only find two examples of handing someone over to Satan in the New Testament. The first example is in First Corinthians; the rest of that story is found in Second Corinthians. We will look at the second one later.

Paul called the Church of Corinth to walk out his judgment on a church member who continued in heinous sin. This man and his father's wife were living in sexual immorality and would not repent. Paul commanded the church, as a body, to deliver "such a one" to Satan for the destruction of the flesh.

How do you think contemporary churches might deal with a church attendee who was living with someone out of wedlock?

How might they deal with same-gender relationships and marriages?

Some Christians and Churches do not see anything wrong with what the Bible calls sin and abomination.

Many would condemn a pastor for being judgmental and condemning if he or she dared suggested kicking someone out of church for ongoing immorality, drunkenness, addiction, etc. Not Paul, however. Remember, Paul was inspired to write more Books in the Bible than anyone else. The Lord of the Church understood the harm it would cause everyone if they ignored sin in the camp or winked at ongoing personal sin. Paul took the sin of immorality as seriously as the Lord does.

Paul understood "a little leaven leavens the whole lump." (1 Corinthians 5:6; Galatians 5:9)

Paul was a tentmaker, not a baker, so why did he talk about leaven? Leaven refers to sin, and if sin goes unchecked among members of a family or church it leads to widespread compromise. Paul was concerned about building people and churches, not perfecting recipes for baking bread.

Paul instructed the Church to hand this man over to Satan.

Why would an apostle command a church to hand someone over to Satan? For the man's good and for the good of the church. This was not something Paul did lightly or independently of the larger church body. He commanded corporate action from the Church Body, working in harmony with Paul's spirit, in the power of The Lord Jesus Christ. Please take a deeper look at it,

📖 In the name of our Lord Jesus Christ, when you are gathered together, along with my spirit, with the power of our Lord Jesus Christ, ⁵ deliver such a one to Satan for the destruction of the flesh, that his spirit may be saved in the day of the Lord Jesus. ⁶ Your glorying *is* not good. Do you not know that a little leaven leavens the whole lump? 1 Corinthians 5:4–6.

Paul instructed the church at Corinth to deliver a member of their congregation over to Satan, because he was living in unrepented sin with his Father's wife. Paul told them to deliver the man to Satan for the destruction of his flesh, so his spirit may be saved.

Many theologians believe this meant Paul told them to expel the man from fellowship with the church. I think it means more than that. There is a time when God wants us to hand someone over to Satan because nothing else had proven effective in destroying their flesh, and saving their spirit.

Threefold purpose in handing the man over to Satan:

a) **For the destruction of his carnal flesh.**

The Bible speaks of being crucified with Christ, so it is no longer we who live, but Christ who lives in us. Jesus repeatedly told seekers, "If you want to come after Me, deny yourself, take up your cross daily, and follow Me." Jesus calls us to do this voluntarily, but when people refuse to follow Jesus the way He calls them to, more desperate action is needed to destroy the flesh. Why is such drastic action needed?

b) **That their spirit may be saved before it is too late.**

Pastors, parents, and church members balk at the idea of not feeding someone if they will not work. They overplay mercy because they don't want prodigals to suffer. People are handed over to Satan to prevent worse and irreversible suffering. Hell is worse than any earthly suffering!

When misplaced compassion gets in the way of God's corrective punishment, prodigals may end up spending eternity in hell where the worm does not die.

c) Removing the leaven (sin) before it destroys others.

Children and church members suffer harm when authority figures give disproportionate attention to wrongdoers to the point they fail to build and encourage those who try to do right.

If schoolteachers give all their attention to those who refuse to learn, those who want to learn will be stunted in their growth and potential.

📖 He who walks with wise men will be wise, But the companion of fools will be destroyed. Proverbs 13:20.

God's ultimate outcome of handing this man over to Satan.

The rest of this man's story, given in 2 Corinthians 2:1–11, shares Paul's heart toward the prodigal when he repents. Most theologians think Paul was referring to the same man he mentioned in 1 Corinthians 5. So, do I. We must never forget the goal of handing people over to Satan is so they will truly become sorry for their sin and repent. The man repented, put away his father's wife, and was welcomed back into the church!

📖 This punishment which *was inflicted* by the majority *is* sufficient for such a man, [7] so that, on the contrary, you *ought* rather to forgive and comfort *him*, lest perhaps such a one be swallowed up with too much sorrow. [8] Therefore I urge you to reaffirm *your* love to him. [9] For to this end I also wrote, that I might put you to the test, whether you are obedient in all things. [10] Now whom you forgive anything, I also *forgive*. For if indeed I have forgiven anything, I have forgiven that one for your sakes in the presence of Christ, [11] lest Satan should take advantage of us; for we are not ignorant of his devices. 2 Corinthians 2:6–11.

This man was handed over to Satan to learn not to blaspheme, his carnal nature was destroyed, and he was lovingly brought back into the family. Isn't that what we want?

As soon as sinners repent, we can and should welcome them back warmly (although limiting their responsibilities until their repentance is evident). Paul encouraged the Corinthians to welcome this repentant sinner back and forgive him and comfort him.

We will look at one other example of handing someone over to Satan. Remember, the goal of handing people over to Satan is so they will truly become sorry for their sin and repent.

Paul instructed Timothy to hand people over to Satan. Not for blatant sin but for damning doctrine.

We must make sure our doctrine is correct before kicking someone out of church if we don't like what they are doing. There is something suspicious about an overweight Believer shunning another Believer because he/she smokes. A doctor told me being more than 20 pounds overweight has similar consequence to smoking a pack of cigarettes a day. Jesus speaks of this when he says we need to take the log out of our eye before we try to remove a splinter from our brother's eye (Matthew 7:5). Again, we must make sure our doctrine is biblical.

I took a Marine through deliverance. He had completed his years of service and was actively involved in a local church. But he struggled with things like anger. His appointment was one of the most memorable I've ever experienced. At one point a mocking spirit of anger rose up and he jumped out of the chair with such force, the chair legs shattered. He came over to hurt me. I commanded him to sit down in a chair with steel legs. Then he tore his shirt, leaving it in shreds. I heard the buttons bouncing off the walls and ceiling. Thankfully, he was delivered before he could hurt me or destroy anything else. He was genuinely embarrassed and sorry for what he had done. Thank God, his journey was not over.

He went back to his Spirit-filled pastor and church and was told if demons were cast out of him, he wasn't saved. He was almost kicked out of church for correct doctrine. Thankfully, his pastor witnessed the change in his life and later commissioned him to minister deliverance to others.

It is so important we rightly divide the Word of Truth, rather than judging others because they think differently than we do. I remember one minister who doesn't believe in deliverance ministry who said, "I will see you in heaven, and when you get there, I will say "See!" I merely answered, "we both do God's will, you in your way, and I in His." Enough of the funny stories.

Paul Charged Timothy to follow his example with prodigals.

📖 This charge I commit to you, son Timothy, according to the prophecies previously made concerning you, that by them you may wage the good warfare, [19] having faith and a good conscience, which some having rejected, concerning the faith have suffered shipwreck, [20] of whom are Hymenaeus and Alexander, whom I delivered to Satan that they may learn not to blaspheme. 1 Timothy 1:18–20.

Paul encouraged Timothy to review previous prophetic words given to him so he might realign with his prophetic destiny and do everything God called him to do. Paul told him to grasp the high calling on his life with courage. It takes intestinal fortitude to follow God's will all the way through, especially when it comes to discipling wayward prodigals.

We can also review prophecies spoken over prodigals. We can use such prophesies to war over their destinies. Many prodigals, like Saul of Tarsus whose name was changed to Paul, have high callings on their lives. It is no wonder Satan tries so hard to destroy them. As soldiers of Christ, we are to war for ourselves, for prodigals, for the church, and our communities and nations.

There were some in the church, then and now, who had rejected faith in Jesus as Lord and Master. They conned their way into churches and some into leadership, pretending to be something good and holy when they were sinful and unruly.

A con is a ruse used deceptively to gain acceptance or to take advantage of others. Remember, we are discussing Prodigals and their behaviors. Satan has conned them into believing they have a right to live however they wish. Their consciences are seared to the point they are not ashamed of shameful living. God prompted me to put a hyphen in the word conscience. CON–SCIENCE.

Hymenaeus and Alexander had seared consciences. Science refers to knowledge, but just as there is spiritual knowledge, there is carnal knowledge. A buzz word in carnal government since 2020 has been "Follow the Science." The problem with that is, too much science is carnal science. People, thinking themselves to be wise have become fools. One of God's attributes is Omniscience. Omni = all, and science = knowledge. God is all knowledge.

Carnal people, from teachers to politicians to counselors and counselees, and parents and prodigals hold science (knowledge) over the Word of The Omniscient God. This is why they promote carnal science which is anti-Christ and contrary to the Word of God. They believe abortion is a means of birth control, children can choose their gender, men can claim to be women and compete unfairly against women, etc. Carnal people from presidents to children in grade school have elevated themselves above God, thinking their "know so" is more trustworthy than God's say so.

I'm part of a Pastor's Prayer call every Tuesday at 2:00 p.m. As I listened to all the prayers recently, the cry of my heart came out. I prayed, Father, we have prayed everything we know how to pray. We have preached the Word, witnessed, humbled ourselves, and prayed for our state and nation. Yet many states and nations promote abomination, punish the righteous and celebrate criminals. I'm convinced there is little more we can do. We need YOU to move. We need YOU to awaken our country. We need YOU to use Your powerful right arm and save our nation.

I believe we can pray for prodigals the same way. We need God to move, but there are times we have to move out of His way first. If Paul had pleaded for the man in 1 Corinthians Chapter 5 to be given another chance, the man and his father's wife might have died in their sin.

Hymenaeus is "one of the some" who put away faith and a good conscience until their faith suffered shipwreck. Paul's reason for handing such prodigals over to Satan is clearly stated: "That they might learn not to blaspheme." It is blasphemous to pretend you are living in victory when sin has so gripped you that you can continue in sin while strutting your spiritual knowledge and giftedness before God and people.

In 2 Timothy 2:17, Paul includes Hymenaeus and Philetus among persons whose profane and vain babblings will increase towards more ungodliness, and whose teaching "will spread as a cancer." In their case, they taught the resurrection had already occurred, even as some contemporary cults do. By handing Hymenaeus and Alexander over to Satan, Paul set the example that false doctrine should never be tolerated.

There is no place in the church for doctrines of demons. I remember two preachers in our minister's association who believed in Universal Reconciliation. They taught everyone will eventually go to heaven, regardless of whether they accept or follow Jesus. I loved them as people but was glad when they quit spewing their poison in our city. Paul emphasized that such teaching must not be allowed. In a nutshell, Hymenaeus had made a public and Christian profession of faith in Christ, yet he had not turned away from evil, but by his profane teaching, he went towards more ungodliness. This led to his abandoning his faith and a good conscience; thus he brought about the end result of his faith—being shipwrecked.

Paul did Hymenaeus and the church a favor by viewing sin as serious as God does.

It isn't easy for parents or pastors to hand a rebellious person over to Satan. It was probably easier for Apostle Paul to take such drastic measures than it was for Timothy and other pastoral people.

I've handed a small number of people over to Satan so they might learn not to blaspheme. They were all professed Christians but refused to either get married or stop living in sin. Those who repented of sin, were salvaged and went on to live productive Christian lives. Those who refused to repent had things go from bad to worse. They were overtaken by sickness, lack, and early death. These things are likely even if they are not handed over to Satan, because, as Romans 6:33 says,

📖 For the wages of sin *is* death, but the gift of God *is* eternal life in Christ Jesus our Lord. Romans 6:23.

When disciplining prodigals, grace says, apply the least evasive form of discipline necessary.

Mercy warns desperate times call for desperate measures.

If you have read thus far in the book, there are probably some prodigals you are concerned about. Remember, God wants to restore them even more than you do. The best chance you have to be successful is to partner with God. Consider Jesus' invitation below.

📖 Come to Me, all *you* who labor and are heavy laden, and I will give you rest. [29] Take My yoke upon you and learn from Me, for I am gentle and lowly in heart, and you will find rest for your souls. [30] For My yoke *is* easy and My burden is light." Matthew 11:28–30.

Take a moment to ask Holy Spirit: "What are you saying to me through this chapter?" Jot down any thoughts He gives you and pray; make them a matter of prayer and meditation.

Prayer: Lord Jesus, I ask You to train my hands for war as I engage with You to see my prodigal(s) return to You. I do bring my heavy burden to You, and take Your yoke so I can learn from You. I choose to walk in partnership with You in all my efforts to turn sinners from the error of their ways. By faith, I receive Your blessing of a quiet and gentle spirit. In Jesus' Name, Amen.

Endnotes:

[1] *I'll Get It.* Fun & Philosophy. The Furrow, Spring 2023.
[2] David C. McCasland wrote the single session Bible Study "*The Severe Mercy of God.*" Posted online January 01, 2005.
[3] Obert Skye, Leven Thumps and the Whispered Secret.

Chapter Fourteen:
Hope for Parents of Prodigals

Jessica Saddler, who has served in Reach the Forgotten for three years, was recently commissioned to be the Head Chaplain of the Branch County (Coldwater Michigan) jail ministry. Her story proves no one is beyond reach if they have someone praying for them.

Dope Dealer to Hope Healer

At the age of 11, I started using drugs. By the age of 14, I was dating an older man who cooked methamphetamines and was very abusive. I got pregnant and had 2 children by the age of 16. By age 22, I was completely broken. I was selling drugs, misusing people, and being abused to the point of death many times. During this time, I was in and out of jail. I had been to jail five times and had no hope. The man I was with caught and sentenced to 25 years in prison. I remembered, at that time I felt I was finally free, and he no longer could hurt me. However, I kept going on the same path which landed me into another toxic relationship.

I started dating one of my best friends' brothers. I thought he was the one. I went to jail at the beginning of our relationship, and he would write back and forth, and he supported me while I was incarcerated.

After I was released, we moved in with each other and had a child (my first baby girl). Life was kind of looking better. Unfortunately, I found myself in the same boat. He wasn't physically abusive but very emotionally abusive to the point I was no longer living; I was chasing him because I thought I could do no better.

I started work at a local restaurant where a local Pastor would come eat breakfast every morning. I didn't pay much attention until he started to build a rapport with me. He would come in and sit in my section and we got to know each other very well. He invited me to church one night. It was a Friday night service, but I told him I had to work. He told me he had already worked that out with my manager and that I could have the night off if I wanted. So, I went.

After I got there, I went all the way to the back and I remembered thinking, "if this 'this stuff' is real, come and get me." The preacher stopped the service and spoke into my life. I had experienced God for the first time. I would like to say everything got better and things were good afterward, but no. Things did not get better for a long time. There were so many things I had to work through—I mean a lot of things. The first thing is, I married the guy I was with.

He started coming to church with me and we were growing our faith together. Things were finally starting to turn around in my life. We were together for 9 years until one day he didn't come home from work. I went looking for him and found him in bed with another woman. God led me straight to where he was. There was my life, my life was over! The man of my dreams, my everything, the person I had started my faith journey with. At that moment I remember thinking. . . well, thinking nothing! I was completely frozen, devastated at the very least.

Well. . . I blamed God. I had done everything I was supposed to up to this point. I believed that God would always protect my marriage from what had just happened. So, I did a thing, I turned back and went back into a life of cooking and selling drugs, only this time I was under deep conviction the whole time.

Keep praying for your loved one. God is hearing you. I would go to church knowing I was not living what I said I was living; I was living a double life. I was so angry at God, because how could God allow this to happen? After all isn't He in charge of everything? Isn't He sovereign? These are things I would openly confess to God. I wasn't even trying to hide how I felt about Him at this point because I thought God turned His back on me like everyone else in my life. I was used to being let down. So, I ran from God. How could God let this happen to me? I started praying that he would come back. I had preachers, elders, and everyone telling me to keep praying he would be back. They would say God will bring him back. Well, I kept praying, praying more and praying until one day God said, "I have shut that door." Wait, but everyone is telling me to keep praying for him back. God said "NO" This made me even angrier. I thought what I wanted and needed was for him to come home. But God knows better! God knows what you need before you know what you need. You can trust God with your life!

After living back in a lifestyle of dope and running the streets my life almost ended. I was in a car with a group of dope cooks, and we were pulled over by the police. Yup, we had drugs and weapons; the driver was driving on a suspended license and was intoxicated. The officers came and pulled us all out of the car and separated us. I asked the officer if I could make a phone call. I called my Pastor and confessed everything I had been doing and how I was living. He said, "I knew." When we think we are hiding we are not. Then he said, "Call me back, I'm going to pray." I thought to myself, *Pray? I'm going to prison; I'm not going to be able to call you*. I hung up and the officer took me over to a hill and sat me down. At this time, I started crying out to God to come help me and rescue my life. This was a conviction I had never felt before. This is where I truly was born again. I had made a vow with the Lord that day. I said "God if you let me go free, I will go get my daughter and will never do drugs again. I will be completely done." I call it my Hill of Damascus. Well, it happened. The officer came and uncuffed me and said I was free to go. What? I'm free to go. Yup, the officer said, you are free to go. He said you might have a warrant out later, but you can go. See what the Lord did supernaturally he also did in the natural. Not only was I let go, but everyone that was in the car that day was also let go, including the driver who was driving on a suspended license and driving while intoxicated. After that, I told them never to contact me again. I moved in with my Sunday school teacher and never looked back.

Many years later, I started praying for a husband. I prayed for 4 years and finally God supernaturally answered me, and we went on our first date and married in less than three months. Our first date was July 4th, and we were married by September 26. When God moves, he moves! And what God joins together no man can separate.

📖 Wherefore they are no more twain, but one flesh. What therefore God hath joined together, let not man put asunder." Matthew 19:6 KJV.

I married the son of the Pastor who led me to the Lord and mentored me all those years. He didn't know he was grooming his future daughter-in-law. God sure does have a personality.

📖 "Remember [carefully] the former things [which I did] from ages past; For I am God, and there is no one else; I am God, and there is no one like Me, [10]Declaring the end and the result from the beginning, And from ancient times the things which have not [yet] been done, Saying, 'My purpose will be established, And I will do all that pleases Me and fulfills My purpose,'" Isaiah 46:9–10 AMP.

Moving forward a couple of years my husband and I left the only church we had known. We both were feeling a call from the Lord into ministry. We prayed and felt God led us to Dexter Lake Church of God. Uniquely this was a church that had a **Ministers in Progress program**. They trained and equipped pastors for ministry. God always has a plan!

After being at this church for 6 months, we were asked if we were like to obtain our ordination for Ministry. My husband and I were blown away; we had no idea they ordained ministers. But God knew and lead us into our destiny. This program was two years long and in the middle of my ordination, God uniquely called me into Jail ministry.

Here is one key I learned during this process. I found out my grandma was a long-time faithful member of the Church of God. All those years I had no idea. I remember her taking us to church with her when we would visit, but to find out that I'm being ordained through the very denomination my grandmother was part of for many years. What! God had a plan. I wonder how many prayers she prayed for me. What is the coincidence? There is no coincidence with God. God had brought full circle into my life what my grandma had sowed into for many years of her life. God is working long after our time here on earth is over. My grandma passed during my time of addiction, so I never had a chance to know her.

  📖 For I know the plans and thoughts that I have for you,' says the Lord, 'plans for peace and well-being and not for disaster to give you a future and a hope. 12Then you will call on Me and you will come and pray to Me, and I will hear [your voice] and I will listen to you. 13Then [with a deep longing] you will seek Me and require Me [as a vital necessity] and [you will] find Me when you search for Me with all your heart." Jeremiah 29:11–13 AMP.

Don't ever stop praying. You might not even see the salvation of your loved one, but just know God is working all things together for those you are praying for.

  📖 "And we know [with great confidence] that God [who is deeply concerned about us] causes all things to work together

[as a plan] for good for those who love God, to those who are called according to His plan and purpose."
Romans 8:28 AMP.

True hope is found in our relationship with Jesus Christ. He is good and good all the time. What the enemy means for harm God will turn it around for our good.

📖 "You intended to harm me, but God intended it all for good. He brought me to this position so I could save the lives of many people." Genesis 50:20 NLT.

Just think of Joseph. If he had stopped in the middle, he would never have received the full blessing which was for his family to be saved. Joseph was able to remain faithful through all his hardship because God was with him.

The coolest part is, I'm now the lead Chaplain at our local sheriff's department. I'm the first woman to serve as lead Chaplain in over 40 years of ministry there. Our God is that big! Nothing can stop what he has predestined!

📖 But Jesus beheld them, and said unto them, With men this is impossible; but with God all things are possible.
Matthew 19:26 KJV.

I'm now leading women and men into the recovery that I received. That recovery is Jesus Christ. Our hope, our redemption, our restoration, everything you will ever need is found in Jesus Christ. You will find your purpose and your destiny. God will restore everything you lost in your addiction.

I don't ever want to end without allowing you to ask God into your heart if you haven't already. And fully surrender your will over to the Lordship of Jesus Christ! Or maybe you have been walking with the Lord for many years and you need to renew your vow with the Lord?

Either way, say this prayer and believe in your heart and you will be saved! It's that easy. It's not by works that you are saved. It is a gift from God. He paid a high price for you! We just have to receive it.

Thank you for bearing my sins and giving me the gift of eternal life. I ask that you come to be the Lord of my life. I ask for you to forgive me for any area of my life that is not pleasing to you. Forgive me Lord Jesus and save me. I believe your words are true. Come into my heart, Lord Jesus, and be my Savior. Amen.

Romans 10: 9–11 says this,

📖 Because if you acknowledge and confess with your mouth that Jesus is Lord [recognizing His power, authority, and majesty as God], and believe in your heart that God raised Him from the dead, you will be saved. For with the heart, a person believes [in Christ as Savior] resulting in his justification [that is, being made righteous--being freed of the guilt of sin and made acceptable to God]; and with the mouth he acknowledges and confesses [his faith openly], resulting in and confirming [his] salvation. For the Scripture says, "Whoever believes in Him [whoever adheres to, trusts in, and relies on Him] will not be disappointed [in his expectations]. Romans 10:9–11 AMP.

Hope is found in the promises God has given us—promises of freedom from sin. We can find so much hope in Scripture through the gift of eternal life made possible through His son,

Jesus Christ. No matter what trials, temptations, or pain we may suffer, we can always hold onto the hope, God extends to us.

In his service!

Jessica Saddler
Chaplain Reach the Forgotten Ministries
Branch County Sheriffs Department
Coldwater, Michigan 49036

Final Thoughts

Each person is ultimately responsible for their actions. Satan, the forever loser, does his best to make the parents of prodigals feel responsible and guilty for their prodigal's behaviors.

My life fell apart in 1987 when my marriage of eighteen years ended. I became the custodial parent of all three children. They too were broken by the breakup of mom's and dad's marriage.

I resigned from the church I pastored when my wife left because I didn't think God could ever use me again after a failed marriage. I didn't know what to do. For a while I worked construction, and then worked third shift in a bakery. That allowed me to be home when the children, ages eleven to sixteen, were awake. Then I began a five-year career as a home supervisor for an alternative treatment home for adults with developmental disabilities and/or mental illness. The work was far easier than pastoring the church and being principal of a Christian School, so I had plenty of time to parent my precious children, keep the house and laundry clean, and make sure they had healthy meals.

I was filled with shame because my marriage failed. Satan, the accuser blamed everything on me. A couple of years later, one of my sons quit school and ran away from home. When he returned, we went for professional counseling. We both shared a lot in our first appointment. The counselor asked me if I felt responsible for every one of my son's wrong decisions. I did! I rehearsed the "if only I would have, could have, should have done" things differently spiel the accuser placed in my mind. She tried her best to convince me my son was responsible for his own choices and decisions. I didn't buy it. I was convinced, with a lot of help from the devil, I was fully to blame for every wrongdoing of my prodigal.

A few months later, I was listening to Chuck Swindoll on the radio while I was building a pole barn at our home. He asked an interesting question, "Do you think God is a perfect parent?" Chuck paused long enough to let his listeners contemplate his question. I sputtered my answer, "Yes, God is a perfect father, but I am to blame for everything going wrong in my children's lives." Then Chuck exhorted us to consider how some of God's children behave. God used that one statement to release me from shame and blame for my prodigal's choices. I finally understood, I am responsible for my own wrong choices, but he is responsible for his. By the way, all my children have turned out to be good and responsible citizens.

I challenge you to let yourself off the hook for your prodigal's choices. Doing so will make you far more successful in winning them back to yourself and the Lord.

Take a moment to ask Holy Spirit: "What are you saying to me through this chapter?" Jot down any thoughts He gives you and pray; make them a matter of prayer and meditation.

Prayer: Father, I ask You to help every reader say "no" to the devil's lies, and yes to the One who remits our sin and assures us, "As far as the east is from the west, so far He removes our sins from us." Help each one to receive Your grace and forgiveness, and give them a fresh deposit of Your love and grace for them. Help each one to address the needs of prodigals with the solid conviction you can use them mightily. Renew their hope, comfort their sorrows, and help them never, never, never give up! In Jesus' powerful name.

ABOUT THE AUTHOR

Douglas E. Carr was born again in 1972 and entered full-time Christian ministry in 1973. He worked very hard at the ministry and every church he pastored grew numerically, even though he lacked the spiritual depth to lead his people from the tree of the knowledge of good and evil into the tree of life.

Doug labored hard, but with limited results, until he broke free from religious bondage and finally began letting Holy Spirit work in him and through him whenever, wherever, and however he was prompted to by God.

It took a personal loss to bring Doug to where he cried out to better know God personally. After fourteen years of ministry, he was broken and left "professional" ministry for five years. For Doug, it took personal failure to help him realize just how wonderful God's love and grace really are.

Doug was restored to pastoral ministry in 1992 and has been on the quest to know and share the love, acceptance, and forgiveness of God Almighty. He has come to know Holy Spirit personally and has a great desire to lead people into freedom and victory.

Now his church is not growing numerically as fast as it used to, but the people are becoming large in the Lord.

God has been good to Doug, blessing him with Pamela, his wonderful wife, helpmate, and partner in ministry since 12-12-93. The very meaning of the numbers (12 represents apostolic and/or governmental fullness) in the date God chose for their wedding was indicative of how they needed to grow together in the ways of Jesus Christ and His Holy Spirit

Doug ministered his first deliverance in the mid-nineties. He soon sensed the call to lead others to freedom and began leading freedom appointments and Free Indeed Seminars.

In 1999, after a forty-day fast, Doug was led to Wagner Leadership Institute where he earned his Masters and Doctorate with proficiencies in Deliverance and Intercession. While taking classes there, he met Barbara Yoder and soon became part of her Breakthrough Apostolic Ministries Network.

Doug is truly blessed with His wife Pamela, and their five children, twenty-four grandchildren, and a growing number of great-grandchildren. Doug and Pam pastor His House Foursquare Church in Sturgis, Michigan, and continue to minister deep healing and deliverance, as well as lead Free Indeed Seminars.

Dr. Carr realizes the need to raise up ministers of deep healing and deliverance who walk in the fullness of the Spirit to bring healing and freedom to those who so desperately need it.

During the Releasing the Glory gathering at Shekinah Regional Training Center, Doug kept hearing *The Great Awakening will bring people into the churches who have tattoos and piercings everywhere you can see and many places you should never see. There will be many who have soul ties beyond numbering from recreational sex. Many have been addicted to so many substances they are now addicted to addiction. It is time for Believers to stop being afraid of the devil and his demons and stand up in faith knowing the devil and his demons are afraid of them!"* With this word came two impressions: 1) We need to cast out the corporate spirit of the fear of the devil and demons. 2) God is waiting for the church to be ready to steward the Great Awakening so none will be lost as in the Jesus Movement. This preparation to steward the Awakening includes preparing a few from every church, or at least every city or neighborhood, to be thorough and effective in Deep Inner Healing and Deliverance.

To that end, Doug led regional "Equipping and Certification Programs" in Northern Indiana with Pastor Michael Peterson, in Eastern Michigan with Apostle Barbara Yoder, Pastor Benjamin Dietrich, and Deborah Combs, and earlier in West Michigan with Pastor Leigh Larson. Since 2022, he has been leading deliverance ministers' intensive programs in Sturgis, Michigan.

Doug and Pam Carr also pastor His House Foursquare Church in Sturgis, Michigan where Pam's greatest call is to release the Presence of God through worship and Doug's greatest call is to equip others to do the work of the ministry through pastoring, seminars, and the equipping program.

The book you hold in your hands is Doug's thirty-first. His books and other resources are available through Amazon.com, or they can be ordered directly from him.

For more information on Doug's ministry
and seminars or links to his books visit:
www.dcfreedomministry.com

RESOURCES BY DR. DOUGLAS E. CARR

Devotionals:
Kingdom Thoughts 101
Kingdom Thoughts 201
Light in the Darkness

Deliverance:
Ask the Doctor about Deliverance
Beat Me Up Spirits
Breaking the Octopus Grip of Addiction
Building on a Sure Foundation After Deliverance
Busting Through to Greater Freedom
Divorced! Obtaining Freedom From The Sun & Moon God. Jeanette Strauss & Doug Carr
Free Indeed ~ Deliverance Ministry
Free Indeed from Root Spirits
From Woe is Me to WOW is He!
Holy Spirit as Counselor
Patterns of Perversity ~ Freedom from Iniquity

Discipleship:
Choosing Kingdom
Defining Moments ~ My Journey Toward the Kingdom
Let's Get Real
Kingdom Abundance

Healing:
Kingdom Perspective: Divine Healing

Names of God – Prayer:
Ancient Keys ~ Special Names

Spiritual Gifts: Of God, Gifts, and Men (3 Vols.):

Ascension Gifts
Motivational Charismata Gifts
Holy Spirit Manifestations

Teaching:
Breakthrough Essentials
Getting to the Dirty Rotten Inner Core
God's Say So versus Man's Know So
Holidays to Shape Your Life and Transform Your Future
Making Abundance a Lifestyle
Parents & Prodigals
Schematics: God's Blueprint vs Satan's Programming
Time to Act – The Enemy Snuck in While We Were Sleeping

Free Indeed Seminars:

- MOD 1 Basic Building Blocks of deliverance
- MOD 2 Deliverance from Curses, Iniquities and the Big Five
- MOD 3 Holy Spirit Mending of Broken Hearts
- MOD 4 Free Indeed From Root Spirits
- MOD 5 From Woe is Me to Wow is He! (CD only)
- MOD 6 Breaking Through to Greater Freedom (Pending)
- MOD 7 Breaking the Octopus Grip of Addiction

Doug Carr Freedom Ministry Contact:
Email FreedomMinister@yahoo.com
Web: www.DCFreedomMinistry.com

Messages

Most of Pastor Doug and Pam's messages are available on YouTube. Browse by date at: His House Church Sturgis.

Made in the USA
Middletown, DE
07 September 2024

60553511R00104